# SEO 2018

## (No Bullsh*t)

# Strategy

## The Ultimate Step-by-Step SEO Book

### Casey Leigh Henry

ISBN: 978-1-64204-363-1

I

*To Andrew for inspiration,*

*Ryan for motivation, &*

*Matt for your dedication.*

# Table of Contents

# Read This Part First

This book is exactly what the title indicates: it's a step-by-step guide that teaches you how to implement an SEO strategy without all the BS.

**I've Ranked Not Two, Not Three, But FOUR TIMES on the First Page of Google for a High-Quality Search Term Using this Strategy:**

# Why This Book Exists:

One of the companies I worked for in an administrative capacity hired an "SEO expert" that promised to raise our company's website to the the first page of Google for our local niche, which was an extremely aggressive and cutthroat market.

$25,000 later, the so-called "SEO expert" proceeded to sabotage our website, rendering it completely useless for over a year using shady, black hat tactics.

Many people and sources make search engine optimization out to be a complicated process that not-just-any-ordinary human could possibly wrap their mind around.

**But they're wrong.** It's just a bunch of BS.

And that's why this book exists: *to debunk all the BS* and provide people like you with a comprehensive, simple, step-by-step guide on SEO so you can avoid being taken advantage of and save $25k.

# What to Expect:

Having built many websites for many years, I volunteered to resurrect our company's website. In a little under 90 days, I turned our website around and had us rocking the first page of Google for many of our highly-competitive market's keywords.

The only true indication that your SEO strategy is working is that the phone is ringing, potential customers are commenting on your web content, you're receiving contact forms from your site, and your sales/service intakes are increasing.

*And that is exactly what we experienced after I implemented the tactics I will take you through in this book.*

Now, you can achieve the aforementioned results by paying for Google AdWords. However, in my company's niche, it was going to cost roughly $150-$300 PER CLICK for most of the keywords.

## Our Law Firm Receives $12K Worth of Traffic for FREE Using this SEO Strategy:

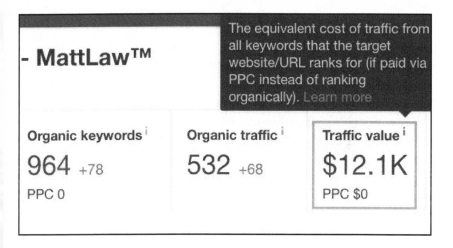

- **MattLaw™**

The equivalent cost of traffic from all keywords that the target website/URL ranks for (if paid via PPC instead of ranking organically). Learn more

| Organic keywords ⁱ | Organic traffic ⁱ | Traffic value ⁱ |
|---|---|---|
| 964 +78 | 532 +68 | $12.1K |
| PPC 0 | | PPC $0 |

Luckily, the SEO strategy outlined in this book will help you achieve results by ranking organically for keywords, which means you won't spend a penny per click on AdWords.

## Here's the deal: it won't be easy.

Not because SEO is as mind-bending as putting a man on the moon.

And not because SEO is as incomprehensible as some mystical, elusive creature that only makes an appearance to those who bring a super secret sacrificial offering to it's super secret lair in the super secret alps of North Korea.

**SEO won't be easy because it takes some hard work, focus, and an honest effort.**

The good news is *most of the hard work has already been done for you* and it's all right here in the palm of your hands (or on your computer screen.)

## Structure of the Guide:

This book is meant to be read chronologically. It opens with all of the foundational requirements your website will need for the SEO strategy to even work.

The first section is called "Preliminary Requirements Check-list," and you need to account for each item on the checklist **before** moving on to the SEO strategy. Otherwise, you are not setting yourself up for success.

The following sections for the SEO process are in logical order. **Each SEO section should be completed in the order they are featured in the book.** That way, the process is implemented properly and you don't get overwhelmed or lost.

Each section starts out with a brief overview followed by a checklist featuring estimated completion times for each step. That way, you know how much time to invest before starting each section.

I recommend keeping this book on hand or next to you as you are actively implementing the SEO strategy. *Again, it's a step-by-step guide that was made to hold your hand through the process:* not merely explain WHAT certain jargon means and WHY it's important.

**This is a HOW-TO book: HOW exactly to implement the SEO strategy.**

# Note on Recommendations:

Before we get started: due to the step-by-step nature of this book, I recommend the use of specific products and services. Most of them are free and the ones that aren't free **are not necessarily required to implement the strategy.**

They are, however, highly recommended because they will make your life easier... and I get kickbacks.

WAIT! Just kidding (kind of.) **Please read carefully:**

I read comments on other SEO strategy guides where some readers complained about the book being *"riddled with recommended products and services that just served to benefit the author."*

So, I want to be up front about the recommended resources I receive kickbacks for: *I don't recommend them because I receive kickbacks.*

I recommend them because I started out using them on my own accord and continue using them for all of my SEO work. **I STILL use every single product and service recommended in this book.**

(By the way, when I say "kickbacks," it's just regular ole' affiliate marketing links - not some kind of corporate back-scratching scheme.)

Keep in mind: **there are free alternatives** to the paid products and services I use (except for hosting services,) and I will mention some of them throughout the book. Otherwise, it's pretty simple to do a quick Google search to find free alternatives and I only want to recommend things I've personally used.

However, one of the step-by-step processes involves setting up an account with SEMrush, which is a paid service. If you choose not to use SEMrush, that's fine.

You can easily skip that section of the process. Google offers a free, less-comprehensive version of what SEMrush offers. *But I will tell you it's not nearly as powerful as SEMrush.*

**These are the PAID services I recommend that I DON'T receive kick-backs for:**

- Cloudflare – cloudflare.com
- Gravity Forms – gravity forms.com
- Upwork – upwork.com
- VaultPress – vaultpress.com
- W3 Total Cache – w3-edge.com/products/w3-total-cache
- Wistia – wistia.com
- Yoast Premium – yoast.com

**These are the FREE services I recommend that I DON'T receive kick-backs for:**

- Ahrefs – ahrefs.com
- AMP – wordpress.org/plugins/amp
- Hemingway App – hemingwayapp.com
- Glue for Yoast SEO & AMP – wordpress.com/plugins/glue-for-yoast-seo-amp
- Google Analytics Dashboard for WordPress – wordpress.org/plugins/google-analytics-dashboard-for-wp
- LinkMiner – pointblankseo.com/linkminer
- SiegeMedia Embed Code Generator – seigemedia.com/embed-code-generator
- Social Media Profiles
- Visme – visme.co
- WP Smush – wordpress.org/plugins/wp-smushit
- WP-Sweep – wordpress.org/plugins/wp-sweep
- WHOIS – whois.icann.org/en
- WordPress – wordpress.org

**These are the PAID services I recommend that I DO receive kick-backs for:**

- SEMrush – semrush.com/?ref=2016101701
- SiteGround – siteground.com
- ThemeForest – themeforest.net/?ref=chenry117
- Ultimate Social – wpsmarter.com/plugins/ultimate-social

At any rate, let's stop wasting time and get to work: **potential customers eagerly await your web presence in Google's search results.**

# Preliminary Requirements:

- ☐ Comfort with Outsourcing (1 Min)
- ☐ Domains (10 Min)
- ☐ Hosting (10-20 Min)
- ☐ WordPress (1-2 Hrs)
- ☐ WordPress Plugins (20-30 Min)
- ☐ Privacy Policy, Terms of Service, Contact Page (1-2 Hrs)
- ☐ Social Media Profiles (30 Min)
- ☐ Google Search Console (10-20 Min)
- ☐ SEMrush (5-10 Min)

In this section, I will briefly touch on all of the building blocks you need to create a strong foundation **to ensure the SEO strategy can operate successfully.**

If you are a beginner, just to forewarn you, *I will breeze through the preliminary checklist items fairly quickly.* Most of the items are straightforward.

If you need more information or background knowledge on any of the items in this section, please remember to outsource using Upwork, or do a quick Google search. (This is a book about how to implement an SEO strategy, not how to build a website.)

## Be Open to Outsourcing

Whether you are a beginner, an expert, or simply strapped for time, **you may need to outsource during the implementation of this strategy.**

# What is Outsourcing?

By outsource, I mean contract out work or hire someone else to complete certain steps for you. If you aren't already comfortable with the idea of outsourcing, *you need to become comfortable with it right here, right now.*

# Why Outsource?

Here's the key to implementing this SEO strategy: if you do not maintain a consistent level of momentum during the implementation of this process, you will not succeed.

One of the biggest culprits of unfinished business is *not completely understanding or knowing what you are doing.* Another huge culprit is *not having enough time.* **Outsourcing is a great way to avoid both of these things.**

Throughout my own implementation of this strategy, I outsourced work and found experts to complete certain parts of the strategy.

So remember: **you need forward momentum and you need to keep going.** *Do not stop.*

# How to Outsource:
Use Upwork. Hands down.

If or when you hit a roadblock, outsource with Upwork. Believe me. It's cheap and there are a lot of seriously talented people around the world who can help you do something as simple as installing an SSL license, or something as complex as this entire process for pennies on the dollar.

Some people prefer other resources for freelancers and that's great. As long as you can locate and hire a talented, competent freelancer to get the work done, *that's all that matters.*

I constantly use Upwork and *it exponentially increases my productivity and efficiency.* So, there's never any excuse to lose momentum in a project or entrepreneurial venture.

If you haven't already, check out Upwork.com, get comfortable with it, and let's proceed.

# Domains

☐ Short & Simple Domain Name
☐ Domain Age
☐ Register Domain for 2+ Years
☐ Public Whois Domain Info
☐ SSL Certificate
☐ HTTPS Domain Application Protocol

## Domain Name

You need a branded domain. Google trusts strong and consistent brand identities more than anything when it comes to domain names.

If you are just getting started, know this: Google cares *marginally* if your domain name has a keyword, but it only gives you a *slight edge for relevancy purposes.*

However, think about your users: make your website's domain name easy to remember and spell. You just need to KISS - **Keep it Short & Simple.**

Exact keyword match domain names can give you an edge if you have *an extremely high-quality site*, but if you don't, the site can be more prone to sinking like a rock ranking-wise. This is due to so many spammy websites having exact keyword match domain names.

# Domain Age

If you have a decent domain name that has existed for a few years and has remained clean without any Google penalties, **an older domain is easier to rank than a brand new one.**

But, it's more difficult to resurrect a dead, dirty domain wrought with penalties.

Domain age is a ranking factor. *However, if you need a clean slate,* by all means, come up with a short, simple domain name and **start from square one.** As time passes, your new domain will age and become more authoritative through this SEO process.

# Domain Registration & WHOIS Data

Whether your domain is brand new or has been around for a few years, **make sure your domain is registered for at least another two years or more.** Domains with registration periods of 2+ years are an indication that it's not spam, and the site owner intends to invest in it.

Google will favor a domain with a registration period of two or more years over one with just a year. *This is especially important if your domain is brand new.*

**Choose a high-quality domain and hosting provider to register your domain with** and avoid high-volume providers.

A high-quality provider that I recommend throughout this book is SiteGround. All of my domains and websites are registered and hosted with SiteGround. If your domain is registered with a high-volume provider like GoDaddy, *it's more likely to be viewed as spam.*

You can easily transfer your domain to another provider.

Choose a new provider (again, SiteGround is amazing) and they can help you complete the transfer process without any hiccups.

## Public WHOIS Data

Make sure your domain WHOIS data is **accurate and public**. Replicate the WHOIS data you provide when registering your domain *onto your contact page*. It will increase your credibility in Google's eyes and they will view you as a real, reliable person versus spam.

You can check to see if your WHOIS data is accurate and public by entering your domain on this website: https://whois.icann.org/en. If it isn't, you can change the information and make it public through your domain registration provider.

A brand new, keyword-rich domain registered for a year with private whois information from a high-volume provider like GoDaddy creates a lot of red flags for Google.

**Get a branded domain, register it for 2+ years with a high-quality provider like SiteGround and have public, accurate WHOIS data to gain credibility off the bat.**

## SSL & Domain Application Protocol

By domain security, I mean having an SSL (secure sockets layer) certificate installed on your website. This will encrypt and protect any data that passes between a user and your website. **It's extremely important to get an SSL if you don't have one already.**

It's easy to do and your hosting provider would be more than happy to assist you. Once you have the SSL installed, it's important to **configure the domain protocol to force all users to access the site via HTTPS instead of HTTP BE-**

**FORE you start building the website.** Or else your website could get funky.

Domain protocol refers to the HTTP versus HTTPS at the beginning of your domain. If you haven't built your website yet, you can add a simple code to your .htaccess folder in your website's file manager to force your website to default to HTTPS when accessed, *regardless of what visitors type into their browser's URL bar.*

For example, if people type in the following variations of your website:
- example.com
- www.example.com
- http://example.com
- http://www.example.com

**When configured correctly, your website will automatically use the HTTPS version when accessed.** It will look something like this at the beginning of browsers' URL bars:

Google prefers secure sites with SSL certificates and HTTPS protocols over unsecure sites without SSL certificates and HTTP protocols.

If you have an existing domain with an existing website that's not configured to force all visitors to HTTPS, *it's usually not worth it to switch.* It's a total pain to change an existing website from HTTP to HTTPS for a slight bump in SEO performance.

**However, you still absolutely need to install an SSL certificate on your website**. Your hosting provider can help you with this task. Even if there's an existing website correlated with your domain, **get an SSL certificate stat.**

# Hosting
☐ Speed
☐ Credibility

You need a high-quality hosting provider. Again, I recommend SiteGround. I use them for all of my websites and they have a great customer service and knowledge team.

Google recently started hosting websites. That may be a good place to start if you have no ties, or if your ties are with GoDaddy or similar.

I've never used Google hosting, I'm pleased with Site-Ground, but *I wouldn't be surprised if Google favored Google-hosted websites in search rankings (for obvious reasons.)* However, that is pure speculation on my part.

**Your site needs to be FAST and CREDIBLE**. Do not use GoDaddy or any of those cheap, high-volume hosting providers.

It's too easy to create spam websites using a cheap, run-of-the-mill provider. *Google takes this into consideration when ranking your website.*

If there were two identical websites, one hosted with GoDaddy and one hosted with SiteGround, Google will favor the SiteGround one purely on credibility and quality.

## Cloudflare CDN

This is a service that delivers your content across a wide array of servers around the world to increase your website speed. CDN strands for Content Delivery Network. **It's safe, secure, and increases the performance of your website for users everywhere.**

If you choose to go with SiteGround, their hosting packages

come with complimentary Cloudflare services. <u>Siteground</u> can help you set your site up properly with Cloudflare.

# WordPress

- ☐ Lean/Clean Site Structure
- ☐ Easy to make updates/changes
- ☐ Mobile Responsive
- ☐ Light Background with Pleasing Color Scheme
- ☐ Clear, easy-to-read Font Style
- ☐ Distinguishable header Styles

If your website is not on WordPress, you need to switch. Hands down.

There are a lot of website platforms and most of them are terrible for SEO (cough cough... WIX.) Some are fine, but I promise you **Wordpress is the easiest, cheapest, cleanest, and most manageable website foundation available.**

*I've never failed with Wordpress.* It may have its follies, but if you approach Wordpress with the knowledge and experience it takes to build a website, you will avoid the pitfalls very easily. Follow this guide and you will stay on the right track.

**Google loves a clean site structure because it can crawl and index your site easily.** WordPress is the cleanest template-based website builder available.

Also, if you pay someone else to build a custom site for you without Wordpress, you are at their mercy for changes, content additions, and all sorts of things. It would essentially become a giant money fire pit and it will cost at least $6K off the bat when done well.

If you are a coder and know how to build a clean site and would prefer to do that, by all means do it. *But WordPress is much faster and will save you countless hours.* **Unless you love doing things the hard way and wasting time and money, I strongly recommend WordPress.**

## Envato's Themeforest

You need to find a WordPress theme to install on your website. I recommend going to ThemeForest and buying one that looks good there. I've used ThemeForest for several years, and they offer a wide variety of great, clean themes to choose from.

Watch out for bloated, bulky themes. *Try to stick with simple-looking ones with enough functionality for your specific web presence.*

**You need a mobile responsive design or your site will not thrive.**

After installing the Wordpress theme, **you need to delete all the preloaded crap.** This includes all plugins, sample pages, media, and comments. Developers preload stuff into themes to show you what it's capable of, *but it just bogs down your site with a bunch of crap you never needed in the first place.*

*Choose your color scheme carefully.* Colors have meanings, but either way, **always have a light colored background. Never a dark colored background.**

There are countless studies that show people are more likely to read your content and stay on your website if you have a light background such as white; or, *I suggest a slightly off-white background.*

**People prefer seeing white space around words because it makes them feel less overwhelmed** and the page looks less crowded. Purely psychological, *but it works.*

I originally used a dark color scheme with light text for one of my websites. However, after reading the studies, I changed the color scheme. *Immediately I noticed an increase in the site's performance and conversion.*

**Also, ensure no HTML or W3C violations exist within your website's coding.** I suggest you utilize an experienced coder throughout this process to look at your website's coding to ensure everything is kosher. Find a freelancer on Upwork if you aren't sure how to do this yourself.

# WordPress Plugins

Once you delete all of the preloaded plugins from your newly installed WordPress theme, you need to download the essential plugins that will aid you in your SEO journey.

Below is a list of WordPress plugins you will need to install to make your website more functional and to track the progress of your SEO efforts. Make sure you enable the plugins when downloaded so they are operational.

- **AMP - support for Accelerated Mobile Pages**

   AMP stands for Accelerated Mobile Pages, which is a project that provides mobile-optimized website content to users that loads instantaneously anywhere on the planet. This plugin is free.

   This WordPress plugin will automatically generate AMP versions for every post you create. **You need this, because otherwise your posts will not stand a chance ranking against content accessed from mobile devices that do have AMP versions.**

- **Google Analytics Dashboard for WP**

  When your Google Analytics account is set up and linked properly to this plugin, it will display real-time statistics for your website on the WordPress dashboard. This plugin is free.

  **The best part about this plugin is that it automatically inserts your tracking code in every page of your website without you having to manually do it.** There have been many times where I created new content, was excited to see how it would perform, then later realized I forgot to put in a Google tracking code.

- **Gravity Forms**

  This is hands down my favorite plugin. It's SO incredibly powerful. Gravity Forms plugin knows no bounds. It allows you to create powerful forms effortlessly and much, much more. This is a paid plugin, but totally worth it.

  At the very least, you need this plugin for lead captures and contact forms. **Gravity Forms can (and most likely will) revolutionize the way you use your website.**

  Without any coding or programming knowledge whatsoever, you can build job applications, employee review forms, product order forms, and almost anything else that comes to mind.

- **Ultimate Social**

  This plugin easily allows your website visitors to share your content on social media platforms. Sharing and engagement from your website proves to Google that people like your content and that it is useful or valuable. This is a low-cost plugin.

Throughout the SEO implementation process, you will learn why it is so important for your content to be shared across the Internet. Ultimate Social plugin will allow your visitors to share your content quickly and easily.

- **VaultPress**

  This plugin protects your content, theme customizations, and plugins with real-time backup and automated security scanning. It costs money, but the peace of mind it creates is invaluable.

  Imagine you finished this book, used the guide, and created a bangin' website... only to have it crash and disappear forever... *leaving you with no choice but to start from scratch.*

  Prevent this from happening with this paid plugin. **VaultPress protects your website from spam, allows you to easily migrate your site, creates real-time automated backups, and lets you restore your website without having to rely on your hosting provider.**

- **W3 Total Cache**

  This is the highest rated and most complete WordPress performance plugin. It will dramatically improve the speed and user experience of your site. The best part is it's free, and you can pay for premium support, but I've never needed to.

  **Remember, if your website is slow, Google will not rank it highly.** Google has a reputation to uphold as the best search provider on the Internet. They want to give people the best content at the highest speed.

Google, and other search providers, *will not sacrifice their reputation for your website* if your site is slow, *even if your content is the best.*

- **WP Smush**

  **This plugin will reduce the size of the image files you upload, which improves the speed and performance of your site.** Large image files put a massive drag on your website's speed. This plugin is free.

  WP Smush scans all the images on your site, optimizes them by removing all the useless data, and finally scales down the image to an appropriate, manageable size.

- **WP-Sweep**

  This plugin lets you clean up unused or duplicated data in your WordPress site. **It removes spam comments, orphaned post meta, and all the stuff you don't think about that bogs down your site performance.**

  It also optimizes your database tables for faster page speed. The plugin is free and does wonders for your website's speed and performance.

- **Yoast SEO Premium**

  This is an all-in-one SEO solution for WordPress that provides on-page content analysis, XML sitemaps, and much more. It has a free version, however, I use and recommend the premium paid version, as it is more robust.

  This is basically a collection of gauges you will check frequently while optimizing your site throughout this guide. It will help you know when you're on the right track and help you stay on the right track. **It's the best SEO WordPress plugin available.**

- **Glue for Yoast SEO & AMP**

  This plugin makes sure all the hard work you put into optimizing your pages carries over to your AMP pages. *Otherwise, the AMP plugin by itself will not grab all the metadata you need to boost your pagerank on mobile phones.*

  **This plugin is free and will significantly improve your content's mobile rankings.**

Other than these 11 plugins listed, I use no more than five additional ones for other specific functions that have less to do with SEO and more to do with conversion goals and online merchant services.

**I highly recommend using the least amount of plugins as possible.** Do not overload your WordPress site with a bunch of crazy plugins or it could bog down your site. One bad plugin could do the trick too.

**So, be careful and do your homework before installing plugins or it could be detrimental to your SEO strategy.**

# Prepare for Google's Mobile-First Index

## What is Google's Mobile-First Index?

You've probably heard your fair share of the importance of having a mobile friendly website. Yes, I know it's a dead horse, but it's about to turn into a zombie horse that will feed upon the living flesh of your website.

*Listen up -*

Google announced last year that they will be switching over to a "mobile-first index."

**Basically, this means the MOBILE version of your website will be considered the ONLY version of your website.**

Whether a user searches from a cell phone, tablet, or a desktop will not matter anymore. The mobile version of websites will show up on desktop and mobile searches.

Say farewell to the desktop version of websites. They will be long gone soon. *You NEED to ensure your website is responsive and mobile-friendly before even bothering with SEO. Otherwise you'll be wasting your time.*

# Why Should I Care About Google's Mobile-First Index?

Currently over 60% of online searches occur via mobile devices and this number is only going to increase over the year. If you have a separate version of your website dedicated to mobile that has more succinct content than the desktop version, then your content's rankings will suffer.

*The full versions of your content on your desktop version will not show up in search results when Google switches to the mobile-first index.*

If your website looks terrible and functions terribly on a mobile device, **you will not stand a chance against competitors on the web.**

*Google's switch can happen any day now, so you NEED to be prepared before embarking on your SEO journey.*

# How to Prepare for Google's Mobile-First Index

**Here's are the three things you need to ensure to brace for Google's Mobile-First Index impact:**

- ☐ Content Consistency Across Desktop & Mobile
- ☐ Have a Responsive Website, NOT a Separate m. Version
- ☐ Easy, Functional Mobile User Experience

## Content Consistency Across Desktop & Mobile

Some websites have mobile versions that hide portions of content to make it easier to navigate and use. For example, you may come across a website with a few lines from an article and a "read more" link that opens the full version of the article.

*If you have a mobile version of your website that restricts the amount of content visible, then the hidden content will not be considered by Google at all.*

**It's crucial to make sure the content visible when accessing your website from a desktop is the same as a mobile query.** It's extremely important, but also a piece of cake to do. Follow the next step!

## Ditch the M. and Create a Responsive Website

The m. or "m dot" stands for a mobile version of a website. For example, if a mobile version existed for this website: https://example.com, the URL would look like this: https://m. example.com. You can see it has a m. or "m dot" in front of the domain name.

**If your website has a separate mobile version, you need to ditch it and opt for a responsive website design.**

You can easily achieve this by going to ThemeForest and selecting a nice responsive wordpress theme for your website.

Which brings us to the final thing to consider regarding mobile-first index…

### Easy, Functional Mobile User Experience

The responsive design of your website it crucial for Google to analyze and consider your content for ranking purposes. **Equally important is your users' ability to navigate seamlessly across your website and engage with the content.**

Be highly conscientious of button sizing, font styles, navigation menus, and social media sharing facets of the responsive design.

*If your users can't run your website on their mobile devices, they will leave your website for a competitor's.*

Google factors the amount of time users spend on your content when ranking it for search results. **Take your time, test out the different available themes, and select one that is easy to read, easy to navigate, and easy all-around.**

# Privacy Policy, Terms of Service, Contact Pages

Once your domain hosting is setup and Wordpress is installed, you need to create these three pages:
- Privacy Policy
- Terms of Service
- Contact Page with WHOIS Data

Privacy Policy and Terms of Service pages are a standard

requirement for any website that wants to be seen as **trustworthy and credible.** *I highly recommend consulting with an attorney when creating these two pages to make sure all the bases are covered for your specific venture.*

There are free options available online to create Privacy Policies and Terms of Service. *However, I still recommend consulting with an attorney.*

**On the contact page of your website, make sure it reflects your WHOIS data** mentioned earlier in this section. When your contact information and WHOIS data match, it's an additional green light for trustworthiness and credibility.

# Social Media Profiles

Below is a list of all the social media profiles you need in order to gain trustworthiness and credibility on the Internet.

- **Google Business**

  You NEED this because it will allow you to show up on Google maps for local clientele. It's also the place where people can leave reviews about your business. Even if you provide products and services around the world, not just locally, you still need to claim your business on Google to establish trustworthiness in Google's eyes.

- **Google+**

  You NEED this because Google made it and they take it seriously (even though nobody else does.) They tried to create a social platform and failed miserably. But since they determine the search engine ranking variables, you should be active on Google+.

- **YouTube**

  You NEED this because Google owns YouTube, and as of a recent update earlier this year, videos from YouTube are ranking on the front page of Google for search queries. I will touch on this later, but I'll leave you with this: it's possible to double-rank on the first page of Google.

- **Facebook Business Page**

  You NEED this because if you don't have a Facebook Business page, you don't exist. Or Google thinks you are weird and illegitimate. Also, you will need to engage in Facebook advertising in this proven SEO strategy.

- **LinkedIn**
  You need this because some people place higher credibility and value on businesses and people that have nice LinkedIn Presences.

- **Twitter**

  You need one because it's additional proof of existence in Google's eyes. Twitter also allows you to engage with potential clients and customers in a unique way.

# Google Search Console (Webmasters)

You need to set up this powerful tool to track your website's performance, as well as identify any issues Google may have with your site that could prevent you from ranking.

The setup process is easier than ever with Google's Webmaster guides and support, which is available in the linked title above.

**To use the Google Keyword Planner tool, you need to enter billing information.** *You also may need to have at least one active paid campaign running with Google Adwords.* This is a new development and has been changing over the past few months.

Access to Google's Keyword Planner tool is essential to the Keyword Strategy section of this guide. So make sure you set it up properly and can access it.

**Once your website is set up on Google's Search Console, you are almost ready to embark on your SEO implementation journey.**

# SEMrush

Last, but not least, you need a tool to track your progress. SEMrush is a paid SEO service. However, you need to spend the money on this tool *so you can actively track where you are ranking for each specific keyword every single day.*

This tool is basically the flashlight you will use to navigate through the dark. **You cannot implement an SEO strategy without a monitoring system that tells you when you need to pivot.** This is my favorite one. I highly recommend it.

Google Search Console, mentioned above, has some of the functionality of SEMrush for free, but it's not nearly enough to see day-by-day trends, among other incredibly powerful information and tools.

# Congratulations!

You've completed the preliminary requirements checklist!
Now you can move on to the SEO strategy.

# Keyword Strategy
Finding the Best Keywords to Rank that Convert into Clients

This section will take you through the keyword selection process. Specifically, we will go into detail about finding keywords to rank for in a highly competitive market.

**Here's an overview of what you will learn, step-by-step, in this section, and the estimated time it will take you to complete each task:**

- ☐ Create Your Keyword List (1-2 Hrs)
- ☐ Prioritize Your Keyword List (10 Min)
- ☐ Keyword Tracking Setup (15 Min)

# Creating Your Keyword List

## What are Long Tail Keywords?

Long tail keywords are the key to rising to the top of Google searches for cutthroat markets that are highly saturated. **They differ from normal keywords in their length and specificity.**

A regular keyword might be "graphic designer." Depending on where you are, the cost of an AdWord for that specific term could be pretty hefty. Ranking organically for that term would be an uphill battle.

**The strategy we will get into will ultimately position you to rank high organically for that short, competitive keyword.**

*But it starts with ranking for long tail keywords first.*

A long tail keyword is any long phrase or question someone would type into Google that would lead to your product or service.

Here are some examples for long tail keywords stemming from the regular keyword "graphic designer":

- "how do I choose a graphic designer"
- "what does a graphic designer do"
- "how much do graphic designers charge"
- "finding a good graphic designer"
- "graphic designer logo examples"

As you can see, long tail keywords consist of entire, or partial, questions or phrases related to the businesses or services you want to attract customers for.

# Why Select Long Tail Keywords?

In our age of advertising, paying for ads that say, "Hey, I'm the best bankruptcy attorney in New York. Hire me! Look how great I am! I went to Harvard," **doesn't cut it anymore.**

## Google Answer Box

One of the most successful features Google has started using in search results is called the Google Answer Box or Rich Snippets. Most of the queries that trigger an answer box response follow a "how" or "what" sentence structure, which creates a long-tail keyword.

The idea behind the concept is to provide a user with a quick and accurate answer to a question without them having to read an entire article. **And it's working beautifully for Google, as click-through rates have increased more than**

**30% when results show up in the answer box.**

Here are a few examples of the answer box in action:

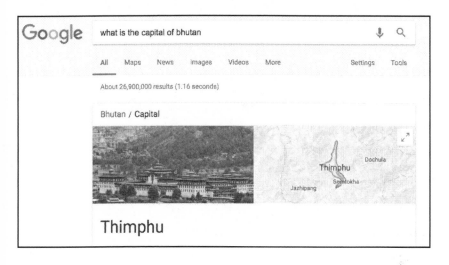

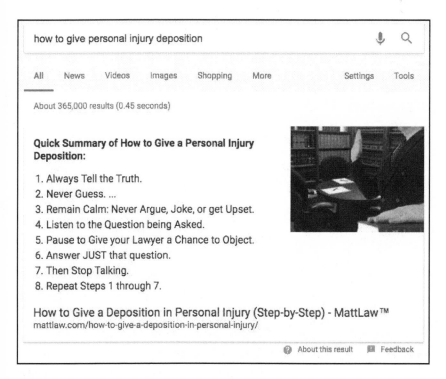

**Most people's search queries are becoming longer and more specific, which is why it is imperative to implement a long-tail keyword strategy.**

## Voice Search

Why are search queries becoming longer and more specific?

*Voice search, the primary culprit, is on the rise.* **It's estimated that 40% of adults conduct at least one voice search per day.**

When people perform a voice search, they tend to use more natural language, resulting in longer queries. (Hence the importance of long-tail keywords, yet again.)

The days of searching for "clarified butter" or "raised garden" are waning fast. **They are being replaced by "how to clarify butter" and "how to make a raised garden bed."** This trend is guiding how Google's AI and machine learning technology ranks search results.

*It's geared toward helping users find more contextualized searches rather than exact keyword matches.*

## Unsaturated Markets

In an unsaturated market, it's easy to rank for simple keywords such as "paintball field Tampa," which was the first website I ever ranked on the top of Google's first page. There are only a few paintball fields in Tampa, so getting on the first page was relatively easy.

As long as you had a website, you were guaranteed to rank on the first two pages of Google. **Sticking to the keyword research process I will teach you in this section will prop your website at the top section of Google in no time.**

# Saturated Markets

In a saturated or highly competitive market like "bankruptcy attorney New York," you would use this same exact keyword research process, *except it will require more creativity in the selection of your keywords.*

For highly competitive markets, you will implement a long tail keyword selection strategy. Let's jump in and learn why you need to adhere to the long tail keyword research strategy:

**People are turning to the internet to answer as many questions as possible before they even think about hiring a professional.** This applies to most product and services purchases.

Once people have maxed out the information they seek, then they will start looking for someone to hire or something to buy.

If you rank on the first page of Google for every possible question they have about bankruptcy in New York, **who do you think they will want to hire or buy from:**

> The guy/gal with a $300 AdWord space at the top of the first page of Google that says "Look at me! I am a bankruptcy attorney! Hire me today!"
> *Or the guy/gal that gave them a ton of free valuable content that answered every single question they posed?*

Also, once you start ranking for a lot of long tail keywords for your business, as a byproduct, *you will automatically start ranking for the short, competitive keywords*, like "bankruptcy lawyer" and "graphic designer" if you follow these steps.

**The best part about ranking organically in Google is that it's free**.

It won't cost you $300 per click.

Another interesting fact is people that tend to scour the internet for answers before hiring or purchasing something tend to be higher quality clientele that will be loyal to you - provided your service or product is high-quality.

**Make sure you are great at what you do.**

Even the biggest, greatest collection of articles that answer every possible question about your service or product *can't outweigh a barrage of negative Google, Facebook, Yelp, and Social Media ratings for not delivering as promised.*

This book will go ahead and assume you are great at what you do and care about your clients. Onward!

# How to Find Long Tail Keywords:

## Generate a Keyword Idea Storm!

**Step 1:** You need to create a list of any and all questions or phrases that come to mind that have to do with your business or service.

I strongly urge you to use Google Sheets, which is like a cloud version of Excel, to create your idea storm.

**Step 2:** In a separate browser tab or window, open up a Google search window. Put your cursor in the search bar and start typing any and all questions relevant to your business that come into your mind.

Watch carefully as *Google automatically tries to pre-fill the search bar with a prediction of what you are typing.*

Everything Google is trying to pre-fill and predict while you type are **frequently searched long tail keywords you need to record in your idea storm.** Check it out:

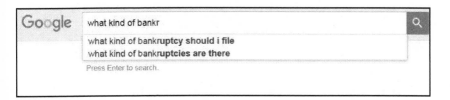

**Step 3:** When you find a relevant question or phrase, type it out in the first column and row in the Google Sheet. List each separate question or phrase in its own separate row under the first column like so:

| Keyword Search Term | | |
|---|---|---|
| What kind of bankruptcy should i file | | |
| What kind of bankruptcies are there | | |

**Pro Tip:** Type as slowly as possible, character-by-character, so you don't miss any of the valuable search terms Google is serving to you on a silver platter.

**Step 4:** With the predicted search query shown previously, click on the top query first. Then, scroll to the bottom of the first page. You will find another precious gift from Google that looks like this:

Guess what these are? Yes. Yes, they are, in fact, more frequently searched long tail keywords to add to your Keyword Idea Storm.

**Step 5: Add them ALL to your Keyword Idea Storm.**

**Step 6:** Go back to the second predicted search term from the first step, "what kind of bankruptcies are there," and search for that term in Google.

Then, scroll down to the bottom of the first page again and add those golden nuggets to your Keyword Idea Storm:

**Step 7:** Repeat steps two through six until you've exhausted *every possible search term.*

Remember to enter all of the search terms you find at the bottom of the first page of Google into the main search bar to find more common search terms at the bottom.

Keep typing in ideas for questions and phrases relevant to your business in the main Google search bar and looking for predictively-filled search terms.

**Step 8:** Just when you thought it was over, there is one more place you can find certain words related to the keyword for your article. These types of words are known as LSI keywords.

LSI stands for "Latent Semantic Indexing" keywords, which is just a fancy term for keywords related to a certain topic. So instead of keyword matching, Google is more interested in topic matching.

An LSI keyword for the video game Halo would be Xbox. Even though the words are completely different, Halo is a video game that is played on the Xbox video game console, as well as computers. So you can see the contextual relationship between them.

LSI keywords should be used in context with your subject matter. The importance of using LSI keywords is becoming more prudent as the underlying artificial intelligence continues to consider search queries in a contextual way, versus exact phrase matching.

To quickly find LSI keywords for your content, use this handy tool from LSI Graph to run a query: https://lsigraph.com/

By the end of the Keyword Idea Storm process, you should have a large number of long tail keyword search terms to work with.

Depending on your niche or market, you will have 10-20 gems, or upwards of 50+. **Get creative and try to think about your products or services in multiple dimensions from multiple angles.**

**Pro-Tip:** How to Find Even MORE Long Tail Keywords:

Fill in the blanks listed below with the product or service you sell. Then, continue with the long tail keyword idea storm steps above.

Whether you are a bankruptcy lawyer, graphic designer, accountant, dentist, or interior decorator, or whether you sell tablecloths, dog collars, wedding dresses, printers, or host events: fill in the blanks with your goods or services.

**Also, think of every alternative name or variation for your profession, product or service.**

For example, lawyers should use the words "lawyer," "attorney," and "advocate." If you sell tablecloths, do searches for "cotton tablecloths," "fancy tablecloths," or "hand-sewn tablecloths."

*You never know what people are looking to spend money on if you don't go find out for yourself.*

- How do you choose a _____
- What does a _____ do
- How does a _____ work
- How much does a _____ cost
- Why should I hire/buy a _____
- Who would need a _____
- What should I expect from a _____
- What kind of _____ is best for _____ (lawyer, bankruptcy) (cleaning product, wood) (accountant, small business owner)
- When should I hire/buy _____
- Where can I find a _____

# Prioritizing Your Keyword List

## What You Need to Prioritize:

Now that you have your long, extensive list of search terms people are typing into Google, it's time to organize the list to meet your needs.

**You need to prioritize the search terms that your potential clients or customers are searching for by search volume.**

## Why You Need to Prioritize the Keywords on Your List:

*You don't want to waste time trying to rank for the keywords people aren't searching for* in your specific market.

What I mean is, if you are a lawyer and you only service clients within a certain radius from your office, then **you need to know what those specific people in that specific radius are searching for on Google and how frequently.**

Or, if you sell a product that's only for women in the United States, then you want to know what women in the United States are searching for, *not men in Canada.*

## How to Prioritize Keywords on Your List:

For this process, you will need to sign in to your Google AdWords account and use the Google Keyword Planner tool.

**As mentioned before in the Preliminary Requirements section: to use the Google Keyword Planner tool, you need to enter billing information.** *You also may need to have at least one active paid campaign running with Google Adwords.*

This is a new development and has been changing over the past few months. Users that have had a Google AdWords account for a while may not have to jump through these hoops.

**Either way, make sure you are setup properly and able to access Google's Keyword Planner tool for the following process.**

If you need to create an active AdWords campaign to access the Keyword Planner tool, quickly create a simple, cheap campaign, run through the following keyword prioritization steps, (shouldn't take you more than 10 minutes or so to complete,) and then inactivate the campaign.

Remember, if at any point you don't feel comfortable with completing any of these steps yourself, **don't stop!** *Keep the momentum going and utilize Upwork to outsource the work so it gets done.*

**Step 1:** Sign in to your Google AdWords account by going to this link:

https://adwords.google.com/KeywordPlanner

**Step 2:** Once you are signed in, you will reach a screen that looks something like this:

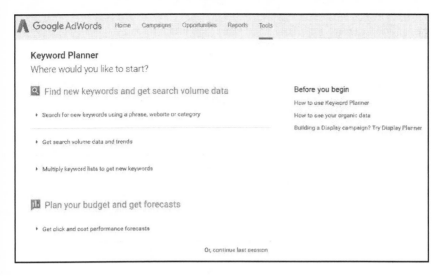

**Step 3:** Click on the "Get search Volume data and Trends" arrow.

Then, copy and paste all of the long tail keywords from your Keyword Idea Storm Google Sheet into the box.

(There is also an option to upload an Excel file if that is what you used to create your list.)

**Step 4:** Under the "Targeting" section, change "All locations" to the area you are willing to service or sell products to.

You can enter a country, city, county, or region. Then, click "Save."

Next, staying in the "Targeting" section, click on "Google." Here, you can choose to only see Google search results, or Google and search partners results.

**Step 5:** Under the "Date range" section, it currently defaults to show the average monthly searches for the last 12 months. I recommend you keep it there.

If you are selling a product or service that didn't exist a year ago or has only recently gained popularity, you may want to see the last six months.

Or, if you are providing a long-standing service, like dentistry, you may want to see the last two years to compare trends. But again, I recommend keeping it at the default of "last 12 months."

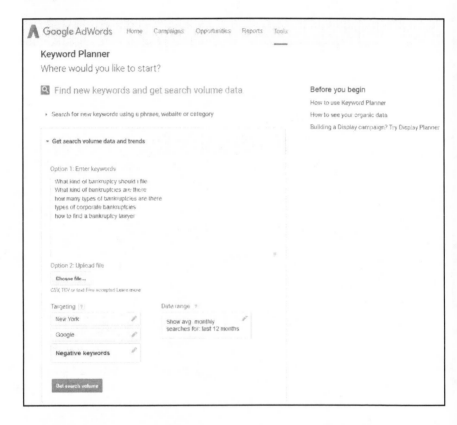

**Step 6:** Once all of the data is entered, click on the "Get search volume" button.

A screen that looks like the example below will appear, **showing you the monthly search volume trends for each long tail keyword search term in your specific area of interest.**

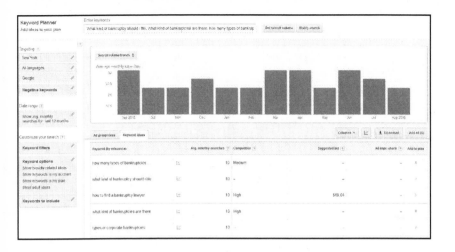

You will notice on the left-hand side of the screen you are able to further specify your market by choosing a language.

(Unless you only service a specific language, I suggest using the original results to continue the keyword research process.)

You can also have Google show broadly related keywords, or customize the search to your liking in other ways. *Modifying your search beyond the instructions listed here is purely up to you.*

If you did your due diligence during your long tail keyword search, then you are at a great starting point.

**Step 7:** Click on the "Avg. monthly searches" box below the graph section, above your first long tail keyword term to sort by the number of average monthly searches.

**The terms with the highest number of average monthly searches will be the content you create first.**

*You want to create the content for the most-searched long tail keywords first to try and capture the most leads right off the bat.*

You will use this list to prioritize which content you work on first. Once you've released your first piece of content, you will refer to this list to know which content to create next.

If there is a batch of keywords that have the same number of monthly searches, then use your discretion to choose what order you want to work on the content.

Any long tail search terms that display a "-" under the "Avg. monthly searches" column means that less than 10 people are searching for that term in your specific area.

*I recommend keeping these terms and working on getting them on your website after the actively searched terms are rocking and rolling.*

You can download the information from the Google Keyword Planner by clicking on the "Download" button to the right, underneath the graph section.

I recommend saving it in your Google Drive to reference while you go through the next steps of creating your content.

# Tracking Keywords for Google Ranking

## What is Keyword Tracking:

Keyword tracking involves watching how keywords related to your website are positioned in Google searches.

As you implement the SEO strategy taught in this book, keyword tracking allows you to watch your keyword's ranking progress over time.

## Why is Keyword Tracking Important:

Keyword Tracking gives you feedback on your website's SEO performance. **The objective is to create content that positions your website at the top of Google searches, where potential customers are likely to see.**

As you create and change content, *keyword tracking will help you gauge which content is performing well and what content needs more attention.*

It's critical to track your website's keyword positions. **Not tracking your keywords is like driving in the dark without headlights or a map.** So let's turn on the headlights and use a map.

## How to Set Up Keyword Tracking:

**Step 1:** If you haven't already, go to <u>https://www.semrush.com/</u> and subscribe to their monthly PRO plan. It allows you to track up to 500 keywords.

Once you are signed up, go to your Dashboard, and on the top bar next to search, click the + sign next to "Projects."

Enter your website domain and a name for the Project. Choose any name you'd like, but make sure the URL you enter in the domain section is accurate. Then click "Create."

**Step 2:** Your Dashboard will show an assortment of tools you can set up to track your website's performance. For this step, we will only set up the "Position tracking" tool. Click on the "Set up" button under the "Position Tracking" box.

A screen will pop up that looks something like this:

(You shouldn't have to mess with the "Advanced settings" unless you need to track a subdomain, URL, or subfolder instead of your root domain.)

**Step 3:** Click on 2, "Location and Device." Under the "Select location" section, make sure you use the same parameters you did while checking the volume and frequency of your search terms in Google Keyword Planner.

Then, under the "Select Device" section, choose "desktop" or "mobile." *It doesn't matter which one you choose right now, because you will repeat these same exact steps and choose the one you didn't choose before.* That way, we can track your desktop and mobile keyword positioning.

**Step 4:** Click on 3, "Competitors." SEMrush will automatically suggest competitors who are competing with your particular product or service both organically and with paid AdWords campaigns. You can choose to add them to your competitors list or not.

You can copy and paste the URLs from competitors that aren't shown on the list that you would like to track as well. You can add up to 20 competitors to track on this feature.

**Make sure you choose the competitors that are actually doing relatively well on the internet or advertising-wise so you can watch your progress against them.**

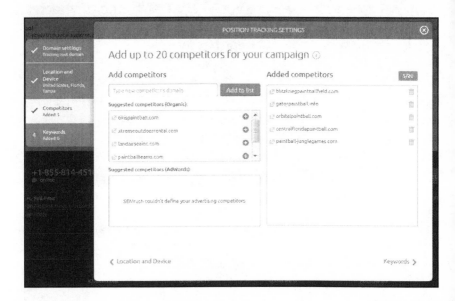

**Step 5:** Click on 4, "Keywords." Next, copy and paste your keywords into the "Sandbox." Then click "Add to project." Or, you can upload a .txt or .cvs file with your keywords. You can add up to 500 keywords.

48

**Step 6:** Once all the keywords you want to track have been entered or uploaded, click on the "Start Tracking" button. You will be brought back to the Dashboard and see a "Your data is gathering..." message until SEMrush has gathered all the necessary data.

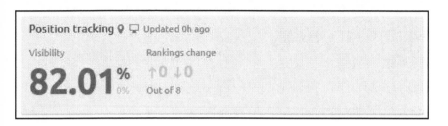

**Step 7:** Once all of the data has been gathered, you will see a "Visibility" percentage number on your position tracking box. Click on the percentage and you will see the screen below:

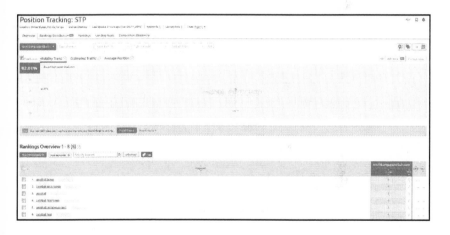

*Don't be alarmed if your percentage is low or even zero.* **We are simply setting up the keyword tracker BEFORE implementing the entire SEO strategy so you can track your progress from beginning to end.**

**Step 8:** Next to your domain name underneath the "Overview" tab, click on the boxes with the dotted-line frames that say "Type domain." Add any competitor's domains from the pre-populated list you want to keep a close eye on. Then, click the green, "OK" button.

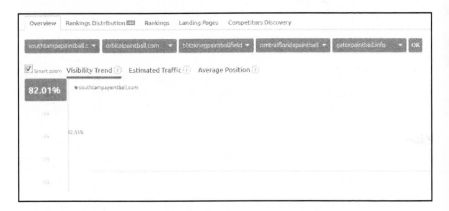

SEMrush will populate the Visibility Trend graph and the Rankings Overview section with your competitor's data. It should look something like this:

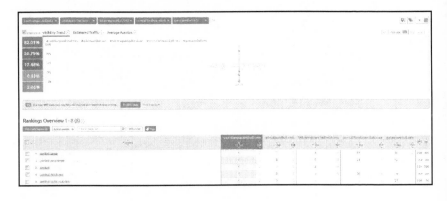

**Step 9:** Repeat Steps 1-9 and choose the "mobile" selection versus the "desktop" in Step 3.

# Congratulations!

The basic keyword tracking setup is complete. Now you can login to <u>SEMrush</u> and click on the percentage button in the "Position Tracker" box on your dashboard to watch your keyword ranking trends against your competitors.

# Content Strategy

Now that you have your keyword list prioritized and keyword tracking in place, it's time to start propelling your website to the top of Google's search results.

**Here's an overview of what you will learn, step-by-step, in this section, and the estimated time it will take you to complete each task per article:**

- ☐ Create the Content (2-5 Hrs)
- ☐ Analyze Content Structure (5 Min)
- ☐ Restructure the Content (1-2 Hrs)

# Content Creation

## What Content Needs to Be Created?

Using the keyword list you generated in the previous chapter, you will create the content for each keyword in the form of an article or blog post.

The content will be what people want to click on after typing the keyword into Google search. *Essentially, the content needs to either answer the keyword question or the content should be about the keyword phrase.*

## Why Does the Content Need to Be Created?

In order to rank for the keywords on your keyword list, **you need to create the content that responds to the queries.**

The mere existence of the keyword question or phrase on your website is not enough to rank for the keyword. Posting pictures pertaining to the keyword doesn't earn your website a spot at the top of Google, either.

**Written content in the form of a guide or article that answers the keyword questions or provides information about the keyword phrase needs to be on your website.** This is how your potential customers are going to find you, and hopefully, choose to do business with you over your competitors.

Remember, in an age of endless advertisements constantly bombarding our consciousness at every waking moment, you need to take the position of being the expert of your product or service and gain new clientele by *providing free, easy-to-understand content about your industry.*

## How to Create the Content:

**Step 1:** Open up your list of keywords and find the one that has the highest average searches per month.

**Step 2:** Create a new Google Doc or Word document. (Again, I highly recommend using Google Docs for everything.)

**Step 3:** Start writing the answer to the long tail keyword question, or write about the long tail keyword phrase. *Yes, if you are not a writer, this will be a daunting task.*

Heck, if you are a writer, this section is going to take some muscle to get through. **In the end, it will all be worth it, trust me.**

Remember, if at any point you don't feel comfortable or qualified or simply don't have the time to invest in writing the content… *outsource, outsource, outsource!* Use Upwork! There are tons of great writers who are willing and able to write all of the content for you.

**Step 4:** While writing the article, try to focus on making it the best possible answer or solution to the question or phrase your long tail keyword represents.

It's one thing to follow all the steps like a robot, but it's another when it comes to the **relevance and quality of content.**

This book will teach you how to rank the content so your potential clients will find it, read it, and buy your product or service. *However, if the content isn't good, doesn't fully answer the question, or isn't engaging, the content will drop like a rock.*

## Making the Content Easy-to-Understand:

As the expert on the product or service you are selling, you should be able and qualified to answer most, if not all, of the questions on your keyword list. **Take the time to craft an easy-to-understand, comprehensive guide for each keyword.**

For complex concepts you need to explain in your articles, *try to use layman terms and create simplified analogies.* Remember, this content is supposed to be for potential clients or people trying to learn about what you are offering.

**Your audience is not your contemporaries or competitors. Your audience is the masses.**

Keep your writing clear, concise, and simple. Take the time to dissect the information and explain all the key parts of the question or topic.

Use simple language. Almost everyone can understand a middle school or high school reading level. **So, aim to create content that could be easily read and understood**

**by an average fourteen-year-old student.** *That way, the content isn't over any of your potential client's heads.*

There is a tool we will use to analyze your content in the next section, and part of it involves using the Flesch readability test. The tool will give your content a *Flesch reading score,* which grades the content based on how difficult it is to read. It ranges from 8th grade reading levels to college graduate levels in grading. You want to make the content easy to read.

Sure, you want to impress potential customers with how smart you are and show them you're an expert in your field, **but prove it with tact and elegance.** *A key part of ranking highly on Google is keeping people on your website reading and engaging with your content.*

If people come across your website and can't understand the answer or solution to the question they asked, *they will simply leave your site and go to your competitor.* **Google takes the amount of time people spend on your website into consideration when ranking your article for a specific keyword.**

Remember that Google is a business too. They want to be the best search engine that gives people the answers they are searching for in the *fastest, easiest, and simplest way possible.* They want to rank the best answer to the keyword at the top.

Sure, Google has other parameters that this book will outline to get your content to the top; but in order for your content to stay at the top, **it needs to engage readers and provide high-quality information.** Otherwise, Google will bury your content as fast as we can surface it throughout this process.

## The Importance of Relevance, Quality, & Uniqueness of the Content:

**Treat each keyword on your list as a title of the ultimate guide on the subject at hand.** Then, become the author. Inform your potential clients. Leave no stone unturned. Don't be afraid to give away gold nuggets of information. Write to the best of your ability.

**Make sure all of the material you write on the subject is relevant.** Try not to jump around to different topics. Keep the article streamlined and in a logical, sequential order. *Remember, the goal is to answer the keyword question in its entirety.*

**Answer it in such a way that someone who clicks on your article doesn't have to go anywhere else for additional information about the inquiry.** The quality and completeness of the article is extremely crucial to the ranking process.

Also, make sure the content is unique and not just scraped from another source. *Be creative and never duplicate existing information on the internet, or else it will negatively affect your website's ranking.*

**Step 5:** Make sure the article is at least 2000 words long. The longer the better. **Almost all the content that ranks on the first page of Google is over 2000 words in length.** Once the content is over 2000 words and was written following the aforementioned guidelines, you are ready to move on to the content analysis section.

# Content Structure Analysis

Now that you have a long, high-quality article written, it's time to restructure the content in a way that makes Google happy. By making Google happy, you will make almost all of your web visitors happy too. Before we start restructuring, we need to analyze the content first.

## What is Content Structure Analysis?

By content structure, I'm referring to the overall layout of the content. **This includes the size of the paragraphs, use of headings and subheadings, length of the sentences, keyword density, and other things we will cover.**

Analysis of the structure involves determining the current state of the content. This will help us figure out what needs to remain the same and what needs to be restructured.

## Why Does the Content Need Structure?

Google has collected a lot of data regarding what people like content-wise on the internet. This is how the ranking system works.

**It was created to figure out what people like, find content that matches the criteria, and serve it to people as quickly and easily as possible.**

Most of the content that ranks highly on Google search results has similar content structures. The methods are easy to replicate. So, instead of reinventing the wheel, **follow the recipe of success by structuring your content in a way that always performs well.**

## How to Analyze the Structure of Your Content:

**Step 1:** If you followed the preliminary checklist at the beginning of the book, you should have WordPress with the

Yoast Premium plugin installed. Login to WordPress, click on "Posts" and then "Add New."

**Step 2:** Copy the entire article and paste it into the content area of the post page in WordPress.

**Step 3:** Scroll down to the bottom of the post page until you reach the "Yoast SEO Premium" section. You will see "Readability" and "Enter your focus keyword" tabs. Get used to this area. You will be spending a lot of time here.

**Step 4:** On the "Enter your focus keyword" tab, type your long tail keyword in the "Focus keyword" text field. Then, you will see something similar to the picture below. This section shows you an analysis of the current state of your content SEO-wise.

In the next steps, I will walk you through the content restructuring process. The goal is to turn most, or ideally all, of the colored circles from red or orange to green.

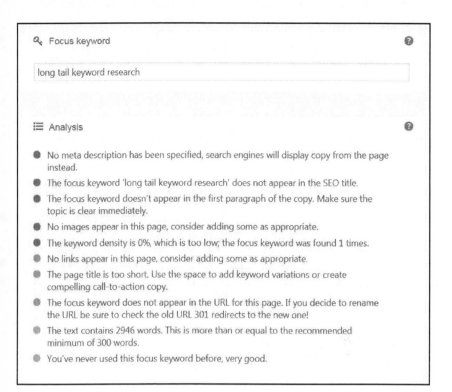

**Step 5:** Click on the "Readability" tab and take a look under the "Analysis" and "Insights" section. You will see something similar to the picture below. This section analyzes how easy or hard your content is to read.

It includes the Flesch reading score we discussed earlier, among other things. In the next steps, I will walk you through the content restructuring process where the goal is also to change the red and orange circles green.

Under the "Insights" section, make sure all of the "Prominent Words" are relevant to the long tail keyword you wrote about. This comes back to importance of the relevancy of your content to the keyword.

**Google takes content relevancy seriously.** If any of the words listed are a little off-topic, you may want to consider revising the content and increasing its focus on the keyword at hand.

**Step 6:** Read through the items listed in the analysis of your content provided in steps 4 and 5. The next section will teach you how to restructure the content efficiently.

# Restructuring the Content

## What is Content Restructuring?

Content restructuring involves molding your article into an easy-to-read format and making it easy for Google to process.

*Examples of content restructuring include breaking up long paragraphs into bite-sized chunks, shortening sentences, and creating subheadings to help the reader.*

## Why Does the Content Need to Be Restructured?

Restructuring the content is crucial to ensuring readers can easily engage with the article. **It also establishes that your article is in a format that jives with Google's search engine.**

If Google is unable to easily figure out all the elements of your content, such as who the author is, what the title is, or what date the article was posted, *the ranking process will take much longer.*

**Structuring the content for Google simultaneously structures the content for your audience as well.** Remember, Google wants to deliver good content to people who use Google's search engine.

## How to Restructure the Content Readability:

This is where all the magic happens. **Once your article goes through this process, you are leaps and bounds ahead of the game.** First we will work on the content's "Readability."

## Reduce Sentence Length

**Step 1:** Cut down the length of any sentences that have over 20 words. You don't need to cut down *all* of the sentences over 20 words long, but try to get the overall percentage of sentences over 20 words long to less than 25%.

If you click on the "eye" symbol next to the Yoast suggestion, it will automatically highlight all of the sentences over 20 words long in your article. This makes the process go faster.

> ● 32.6% of the sentences contain more than 20 words, which is more than the recommended maximum of 25%. Try to shorten the sentences.

## Vary Consecutive Sentences

**Step 2:** Change the beginning of any consecutive sentences that start with the same word or phrase. Keep the content interesting and engaging.

You can click on the "eye" symbol next to the Yoast suggestion and it will automatically highlight any consecutive sentences that start with the same word.

> ● The text contains 2 instances where 3 or more consecutive sentences start with the same word. Try to mix things up!

## Break Up Paragraphs

**Step 3:** Break up any paragraphs over 150 words. Readers can become easily overwhelmed when there's not a lot of "white space" between bits of information.

**Long paragraphs tend to cause people to leave your content and search for a simpler, more concise looking answer.**

Try to create breaks in paragraphs where new information or new thoughts are introduced. As you continue to write more articles, *you will get into the habit of creating short paragraphs and it will come naturally.*

Again, clicking on the "eye" symbol next to the Yoast suggestion highlights the paragraphs over 150 words long in your article.

> 2 of the paragraphs contain more than the recommended maximum of 150 words. Are you sure all information within each of these paragraphs is about the same topic, and therefore belongs in a single paragraph?

## Insert Compelling Subheadings

**Step 4:** Insert appropriate subheadings throughout the article. **There should only be ONE H1 heading, which is the main heading, for your article.** It will be the title of your article and we will cover that in a later step.

In this step, focus on inserting H2, H3, and, if necessary, H4 subheadings. You can add subheadings by clicking on the "Paragraph" drop down menu on the WordPress editor here:

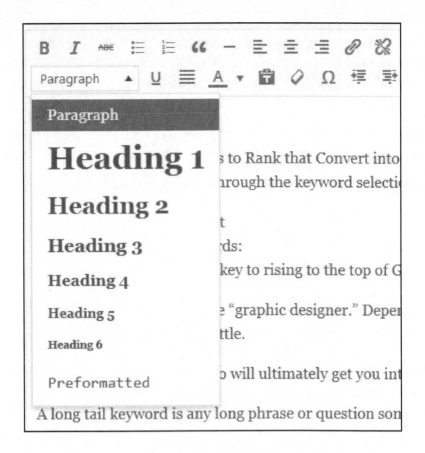

DO NOT USE "Heading 1," because this will be automatically attributed to the title of your article, which will be covered in a later step.

**Try to put subheadings between batches of sentences so there are no more than 300 words following each subheading.** This creates a strong, engaging content structure that performs well.

- The amount of words following each of the subheadings doesn't exceed the recommended maximum of 300 words, which is great.

Type out a short, engaging subtitle using the H2 subheading between paragraphs where new information is presented.

Use keywords in the subheadings where it is natural. *Do not overuse keywords in the titles, but try to use them in sub-headings when possible.* This is a minor ranking factor:

> ● The focus keyword appears in 4 (out of 25) subheadings in the copy. While not a major ranking factor, this is beneficial.

When there is another fork in the logical discourse of your article between H2 subheadings, use the H3 subheading to break up the content even further. **When creating subheadings, you want them to keep the reader reading.** Use them like a little food or candy trail in cartoons to keep readers moving through your content.

When readers are engaged and stay on your article for a long time, it's a sign for Google that your content is high-quality, relevant, and answers the long tail keyword query.

Here's a sample list of subheadings you can use to keep your readers reading:

- Here's the Deal
- But Here's the Kicker
- Here's the Bottom Line
- Want to Know the Best Part?
- That's Not All
- What's the Catch?
- Listen to This
- The Truth Is

Here's a snippet from an article that shows the use of H2, H3, and H4 subheadings:

# Change Passive Voice to Active

**Step 5:** Change any sentences that contain the passive voice into the active voice if the percentage of passive voice exceeds 10% of the overall content. As usual, click on the "eye" symbol next to the Yoast suggestion to automatically highlight sentences that contain the passive voice.

20% of the sentences contain passive voice, which is more than the recommended maximum of 10%. Try to use their active counterparts.

**The passive voice is harder to read and understand than the active voice.** Here is a simple example of a sentence containing passive voice versus active voice:

- The car was washed by dad.
- Dad washed the car.

There is a great article that goes into depth about the mechanics of passive voice written by Yoast. You can read it to gain more understanding about how the passive voice is detected and why you should avoid it: https://kb.yoast.com/kb/passive-voice/

A helpful, free online application called Hemingway App can help you identify instances where the passive voice exists more specifically than the Yoast app. This application also helps you identify sentences that are hard to read, which jives with the content structure in this guide.

## Increase Transition Words

**Step 6:** Ensure that your content includes enough transition words to make up at least 30% of the overall content. **A transition word is a way a writer can guide the reader through the content.**

It signals to the reader if you are explaining something sequentially, if a cause-and-effect relationship exists between the sentences, or if you are comparing something.

Remember to click on the "eye" symbol next to the Yoast suggestion to highlight instances where a transition word exists in your content.

---

12% of the sentences contain a transition word or phrase, which is less than the recommended minimum of 30%.

---

Some examples of transition words include: "and, because, since, while, therefore, almost," etc. Words that indicate the relationship between consecutive sentences are typically transition words. It makes it easier for readers to follow your explanations and train of thought throughout the content.

## Simplify Vocabulary for Readability

**Step 7:** Ensure that your content has a Flesch reading ease test score of 60 or higher. **The Flesch readability tests use the length of the sentences and amount of syllables per word from your content to calculate how easy or hard it is to read.**

A score between 60-70 is typically understood well by 13- to 15-year-old students, while scores of 90-100 are understood by 11-year-old students. Scores 59 and below are best understood by college and graduate students.

You can view your content's Flesch reading ease score in the Yoast "Readability" section here:

> ● The copy scores 70.1 in the Flesch Reading Ease test, which is considered fairly easy to read.

Replace longer words with short words to reduce the number of syllables. For example, instead of saying "sophisticated software," say "complex software." "Sophisticated" has five syllables, while "complex" only has two syllables.

Coupled with the reduction of sentence length in step 1, your content should have a decent Flesch reading ease test score.

## Create a Bullet List or Short Summary

**Step 8:** Create a short summary of the entire article to insert at the beginning. That way, when readers land on your web page, they will know what is in store.

**More importantly, this will increase your chance of showing up in a google answer box, knowledge graph, or featured snippet.** Feature the question and a one-sentence, in-a-nutshell answer to the question. If it's a how-to list of steps, make sure your H1 header is the targeted search term and the list is in a numbered or bulleted format.

Typically, you want to give them enough information to orient them on what your article will cover, **while simultaneously piquing their interest to encourage them to read the entire article.** Here is an example of a summary that appears at the beginning of an article:

## Quick Summary of How to Deal with Insurance Adjusters:

1. Find Out which Insurance Company the Adjuster Represents.
2. If they are from your own Insurance Company, you have a Duty to Cooperate with them.
3. If they Represent the other Party's Insurance Company, be Careful –
4. Do Not Speak to other Adjuster Directly. Have a Friend or Lawyer Speak to them.
5. Do Not give the Other Side a Recorded Statement.
6. Do Not Sign any Documents from the Other Insurance Adjuster.
7. Do Not Settle Your Claim too Quickly.
8. Consult with an Experienced Personal Injury Lawyer to Protect Your Rights.

This example features a simple, chronological guide that summarizes what the article is about. Each point gives a small bit of information without an explanation of "why," **which should cause the reader to want to read the article and find out "why" they shouldn't "give the other side a recorded statement."**

Use the above example as a guide to create your own short summary of the article featured on your website to encourage visitors to read the entire article. After completing these steps, you should see something similar to the following under the Yoast Readability Analysis Section:

**The more green circles, the easier your content is to read and understand.**

# How to Restructure the Content to Improve Keyword Ranking:

## Create Keyword Title

**Step 1:** Create a title for the content that contains the long tail keyword with compelling text. There are four things you should include in your titles:

1. The long tail keyword at the beginning of the title
2. Followed by compelling, call-to-action text
3. With brackets or parentheses
4. Use odd numbers for content with lists or steps

Let's assume your long tail keyword is "how to choose a piano teacher." **Make sure the keyword is the beginning of the title.** When done correctly, you will see this indication under the Yoast Analysis Section:

Next, your keyword should be followed by compelling text that calls readers to action. This includes words that **communicate to potential readers that your content is easy to understand, comprehensive, and/or a quick answer or solution.**

A few examples of effective titles for an article with the keyword, "how to choose a piano teacher" includes:

- How to Choose a Piano Teacher Step-by-Step Guide
- How to Choose a Piano Teacher Right Now
- How to Choose a Piano Teacher Quick Article
- How to Choose a Piano Teacher Ultimate Guide
- How to Choose a Piano Teacher The Real Story

See how "step-by-step" indicates to the reader that it's a comprehensive guide? Also, by using the words "Right Now" and "Quick," this signals to the reader your article is a fast answer or solution to their inquiry.

Using the phrase "Ultimate Guide" tells the reader it's an all-inclusive answer to their question. "The Real Story" suggests that there may be a lot of false or misleading information about the subject and your article debunks it.

Now that you have a title featuring the focus keyword and compelling text, you need to add parentheses. Studies show that titles with brackets or parentheses are 38% more likely to get clicked on than titles without them. Here are some examples of how to add brackets or parentheses:

- How to Choose a Piano Teacher (Step-by-Step Guide)
- How to Choose a Piano Teacher [Right Now]
- How to Choose a Piano Teacher (Quick Article)
- How to Choose a Piano Teacher [The Ultimate Guide]
- How to Choose a Piano Teacher (The Real Story)

Make sure you add the parentheses to the middle or end of the title. Do not add parentheses to the beginning of the title. Google doesn't like that.

Last, but not least, include odd numbers in your titles if your content can be broken down into steps or a numbered list. Titles with numbers have a 36% higher chance of getting clicked on.

Numbers cause titles to perform better because people know exactly how many steps or bits of information are in store before clicking on the link. Here are some examples of titles with numbers:

- How to Choose a Piano Teacher (7 Easy Steps)
- How to Choose a Piano Teacher (3 Simple Keys)
- How to Choose a Piano Teacher (11 Secrets on the Real Story)
- How to Choose a Piano Teacher (5 Proven Strategies)

**Step 2:** Click "Edit Snippet" in the Yoast Section under the tab that shows your keyword. Type the title you created into the SEO Title Section here:

SEO title

Long Tail Keyword Research Guide (5 Simple Steps)

**Make sure the title is more than 40 characters long, but shorter than 60 characters.** After typing in the title, if the colored bar beneath the SEO title field is green, then your title is a good length.

The length of your title is important to ensure it doesn't run off the page on Google Search results. Under the Yoast Analysis Section, you will also see this as an indication your title is the proper length:

⬤ The page title has a nice length.

**Step 3:** Once the title is at a good length, copy and paste it into the title field at the top of the WordPress post editor here:

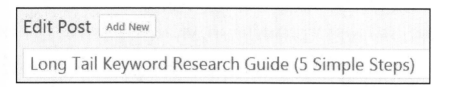

This will automatically make the title of your post an H1, or Heading 1, format. Remember, there should only be one H1 heading in a single post.

## Create Keyword URL or Slug

**Step 4:** Go to the "Slug" field in the "Edit snippet" section of the Yoast Analysis and type in your long tail keyword with hyphens (-) between each word. Here is an example:

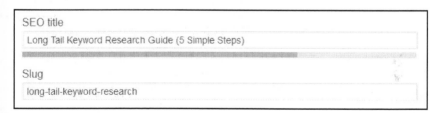

When done correctly, the following text will appear under the Yoast Analysis section:

⬤ The focus keyword appears in the URL for this page.

*Note: if your long tail keyword contains common words in the English language like "to," "how," "do," "it", or other sim-*

*ilar words known as "stop words," you will see the following indication under the Yoast Analysis section:*

> The slug for this page contains stop words, consider removing them.

This warning helps to make sure your URL or slug isn't too lengthy. If I have a long tail keyword that is very lengthy, I will remove some of the stop words in the slug.

If you do not use your exact keyword in the URL or slug, you will see the following text under the Yoast analysis section:

> The focus keyword does not appear in the URL for this page. If you decide to rename the URL be sure to check the old URL 301 redirects to the new one!

If your keyword is extremely long and wouldn't look good or fit nicely in a social media post, it's best to remove any stop words. **A short, concise URL or slug with most of the keywords from the long tail phrase is better than a long, awkward-looking one.**

For example, if your keyword is "how to find a ghostwriter," a shorter, cleaner alternative to the URL "how-to-find-a-ghost-writer," would be "find-ghostwriter."

*Use these tips and your discretion to determine the most appropriate URL or slug for your long tail keyword article.*

## Create Keyword Meta Description

**Step 5:** In the "Meta description" box in the "Edit snippet" section of Yoast, type in a compelling description of your article. **The objective is to coax or convince people searching your keyword on the internet to click on your link instead of your competitor.**

Here is an example of a meta description for the long tail keyword "how to find a doctor after a sports injury:"

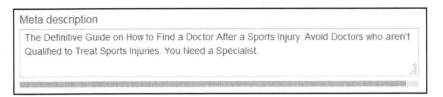

Meta description

The Definitive Guide on How to Find a Doctor After a Sports Injury. Avoid Doctors who aren't Qualified to Treat Sports Injuries. You Need a Specialist.

This process is similar to the title-creation process. *You want to use language that compels a person to click on your link to read your content.*

"Definitive Guide" communicates to the reader that your content is authoritative.

"Avoid Doctors who aren't Qualified," plants into the reader's mind that many doctors may not be qualified to treat sports injuries.

People love to learn things they should avoid or shouldn't do. "You Need a Specialist," makes readers wonder how to recognize a specialist.

Here is another example of a Meta Description that contains compelling language:

Meta description

Quick & Easy Guide on Chapter 11 Bankruptcy for Corporations. Learn the Laws that Affect Your Ability to File for Bankruptcy to Protect Your Rights.

Notice the colored bar below the "Meta description" text field. Always ensure the bar is green. The green color of the bar indicates the length of the meta description is appropriate and not too long or short. **If your meta description is too long, only part of the description will be visible on Google's Search results.**

Use of the words "Quick & Easy" are great in meta descriptions because people would rather have their questions answered quickly in a simple manner.

"Protect Your Rights" would be appealing to an audience because it offers the benefit of learning how to protect themselves from reading your content.

**Make sure whatever you say in your meta description reflects what your content will offer a reader as accurately as possible.**

If people choose to read your article over someone else's because of what was written in your meta description, that's great! *But if you don't deliver on the promise you made in the meta description, readers won't stick around and it will hurt your article's ranking.*

## Check Out Competitors' AdWords Campaigns

**Step 6:** Almost everyone who buys expensive Google Adwords paid for a deep analysis of wording that converts well.

Let's assume you are a financial advisor. Now, type "financial advisor" into a Google Search. Look at the paid Google Ad-Words at the top of the search results. They will look something like this:

Notice all the action-words they utilize in their advertisements. "Gain Financial Insight," "Grow Your Knowledge," "Focus on Retirement," "Partner with an Advisor," and "Minimize your taxes."

Look at some of the offers they include, like "No-Risk Free Consultation," and "Assess your protection."

**These advertisements went through extensive A/B testing and were carefully crafted to convert readers into customers.** You need to search for the top competitors in your industry, find their Google AdWord campaigns, and **mimic them.**

*Don't copy them word-for-word, but make your meta descriptions similar.*

Don't waste your own money A/B testing meta descriptions

or hiring marketing experts. Your competition already paid the bill. *Take advantage of the free sources of information available right at your fingertips.*

When your meta description is the proper length and includes your keyword, you will see this notification under the Yoast Analysis section:

> ● The meta description contains the focus keyword.
> ● In the specified meta description, consider: How does it compare to the competition? Could it be made more appealing?

## Increase Keyword Density

The frequency and placement of your keyword within the content is extremely crucial. You may see something similar from the Yoast Analysis section that looks like this:

> ● The focus keyword doesn't appear in the first paragraph of the copy. Make sure the topic is clear immediately.

> ● The keyword density is 0.2%, which is too low; the focus keyword was found 6 times.

**Step 7:** Insert your long tail keyword into the first paragraph of the article. This is relatively simple. When done correctly, you will see this notification under the Yoast Analysis section:

> ● The focus keyword appears in the first paragraph of the copy.

**Step 8:** Increase the number of times your keyword shows up throughout the article **in a natural, appropriate way.**

*If done the wrong way, this step could cause serious ranking issues.* For example, if your long tail keyword was "how to make gingerbread cookies," a bad way of increasing the keyword density would be something like this:

"This is guide on how to make gingerbread cookies. My family has passed down this recipe on how to make gingerbread cookies for over 100 years. Learning how to make gingerbread cookies is fun and easy. Once you learn how to make gingerbread cookies, your life will never be the same."

This example shows an obvious overuse of the keyword. **Readers will not enjoy the content and you will be penalized for it.** Since your content is over 2000 words in length, you shouldn't run into this scenario while increasing the keyword density.

*Lace the keyword into places where it is necessary and places where it sounds natural.* Try to space out the occurrences of the keyword as much as possible throughout the article. After each addition of a keyword, check back with the Yoast Analysis section.

Add one additional instance of the keyword and check the Yoast Analysis. **For a 2000 word article, it usually comes close to 12 instances of the keyword for a keyword density sweet spot of 0.6%.** Continue adding one at a time until you get the green circle of perfection that looks like this:

The keyword density is 0.7%, which is great: the focus keyword was found 15 times.

## Insert Internal Links

Within each article, you should include links to other relevant articles on your website. For example, let's say you are a writing an article about the different kinds of retirement options available and you have an entire, extensive article about IRA's on your website.

When you mention IRA's in your article about retirement, you can say something like, "For more information about IRA's, click here to read my comprehensive guide about IRA's." Then insert a link in the "click here" link in the sentence.

*Note: it helps your ranking to use keywords from the other article you are linking to instead of highlighting the "click here" text. HOWEVER, it's a bit risky to do it every single time.*

Many scammy websites use keywords to link to internal and external content. **So, extensive use of the technique is a red flag.**

I recommend, again, to highlight what sounds most natural. Sometimes it might be "click here to read more," or it might be, "for more information, you can read my guide about how to start a Roth IRA."

**Again, be careful and always do what's natural.**

**Step 9:** Identify any content within your article that you can link to other articles on your website. Try to find and link at least one. **Ideally, around 3 to 5 would be best.** Only link the content if it is relevant, though.

**Step 10:** Create a hyperlink in the article that links to the other related article on your website. Creating a link to internal content is extremely easy on WordPress.
- First, highlight the text you wish to make a hyperlink.
- Then, scroll up to the WordPress Editor and click the chainlink graphic on the toolbar like this:

- Next, start typing the title of the related article you want to link into the text field like this:

- Click on the article and then click on the blue arrow to finish the internal linking process.

**Step 11:** Repeat Steps 9 & 10 until all the relevant content from other articles on your website is linked.

**Internal linking is crucial to keeping potential customers on your website and reading more of your content.** The more information your readers know is on your website, the more likely they will stick around.

*Eventually, you will become the expert in their eyes.*

**Answering all of the questions they have on a particular subject will increase your credibility and trustworthiness.** It will also keep your website content organized and connected.

## High-Quality, Unique Pictures

**Step 12:** Create a unique, high-quality picture for the article's featured image. The featured image will automatically populate when the article is shared on social media.

Articles with high-quality images are statistically more likely to get clicked on and engage readers than one without an image.

Do not use a stock image. Do not buy an image that others can easily buy and use. Do not use a low-quality, pixelated, or irrelevant image for the article. **You need a unique, high-quality image that cannot otherwise be found on Google currently.**

You can create a unique, high-quality image in a number of ways:

- Take your own photographs
- Hire a photographer to take photographs for you
- Find images online and make them unique via Photoshop
- Hire someone on Upwork to create unique images for you
- Try Visma, it's a free visual image creator with templates

You need at least one image to be the featured image for the article.

**Step 13:** Once the unique, high-quality, relevant image has been created, rename the image's filename to your article's keyword. For example, if your article's keyword is "how to start a roth IRA," then name the image file "how to start a roth IRA.jpg"

**This is a crucial step. Make sure the article's featured image filename is the keyword.**

**Step 14:** Set the featured image for your article. Doing this on WordPress is very easy. Scroll down and look on the right side of the WordPress Editor and you will see a "Featured Image" section. Click on the "Set Featured Image" link:

Then, Upload the image to your media library by clicking the "Upload Files" tab. Click the "Select Files" button. Choose the photograph file to upload from your directory. Then click "Open."

The following option menu will appear:

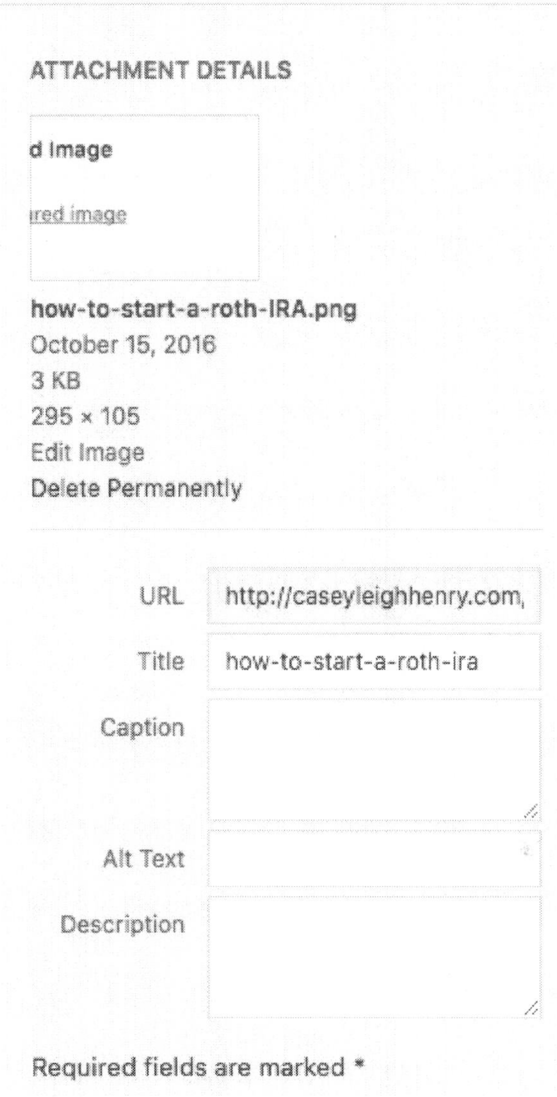

ATTACHMENT DETAILS

d Image

ired image

**how-to-start-a-roth-IRA.png**
October 15, 2016
3 KB
295 × 105
Edit Image
Delete Permanently

| | |
|---|---|
| URL | http://caseyleighhenry.com, |
| Title | how-to-start-a-roth-ira |
| Caption | |
| Alt Text | |
| Description | |

Required fields are marked *

**Step 15:** Fill in the "Caption," "Alt Text," and "Description" fields with the keyword. You can add other things like, "how to start a roth IRA featured image." Just make sure the entire keyword is in each field.

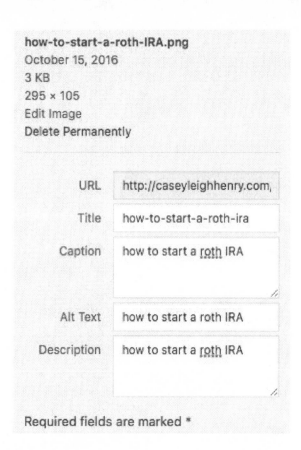

how-to-start-a-roth-IRA.png
October 15, 2016
3 KB
295 × 105
Edit Image
Delete Permanently

| URL | http://caseyleighhenry.com/ |
| Title | how-to-start-a-roth-ira |
| Caption | how to start a roth IRA |
| Alt Text | how to start a roth IRA |
| Description | how to start a roth IRA |

Required fields are marked *

When done correctly, the following text will appear under the Yoast Analysis section:

> ● The images on this page contain alt attributes with the focus keyword.

When possible, add a few more images to the article to engage the readers. **It's absolutely necessary to have one image as the featured image.** Additional pictures laced throughout the article will keep readers on your web page longer, while increasing the article's authority and quality in Google's eyes.

# High-Quality, Unique Videos

**Step 16:** If you are able to create high-quality videos for any of your content, *DO IT!* Google rewards web pages that have a variety of media, such as pictures and videos. Uploading the video to YouTube and embedding the video into your web page works, *but it's not the best way.*

When you embed the video on your website, YouTube includes links that will take your readers to YouTube... *AWAY from your article.* This technique is a double-edged sword.

There's a special and specific way to upload videos to YouTube that will get you on the first page of Google for your keywords. This step-by-step process is in another section of this book.

For this specific section we will only discuss how to use video media on your webpage to increase your article's ranking while keeping the reader on your page. **Remember, a variety of high-quality media like pictures, videos, and infographics is key to your article's ranking.**

If you have videos to use on your web page, use Wistia to host your videos. Hosting videos on your own website will slow down your site, which will kill any chance you may have to rank high on Google.

Remember, Google wants to give readers FAST answers, not answers that take forever to load.

Wistia is a great service that allows you to easily implement video marketing in your articles *WITHOUT any links that take readers off your page to YouTube.* It also has marketing tools and analytics you can use to track conversions.

Using Wistia also allows you to restrict which domains your video can be shown on, which ensures no one can steal and use your video on their own website without your consent. It also allows you to optimize the video to show up in search results.

# Freshness of Content

**Step 17:** Keep the content fresh. How? If there is any updated information related to new laws, recent news stories, or any changes to the information in your article, do this: add the information, and at the beginning of the article, put: "Updated on (date) with added information related to recent changes in (law, policy, etc.)"

Then, change the publish date of the post to the day you updated it. You can do this in the WordPress post editor by clicking "Edit" under the "Publish" section next to "Published on," which is here:

Then click "OK" to save the changes. Google prefers to feed people the most up-to-date, high-quality information on search results. By keeping the content you worked hard to create fresh, it will continue ranking highly in Google's search results.

**Removing or adding entire sections of content to your blog post or article has a more significant positive effect on ranking** than switching around a few words or sentences.

*So make sure you are actually freshening up the content by pruning old information and adding new, relevant information.*

# Repeat the Content Strategy Process

Repeat these steps for each and every long tail keyword you collected in the keyword strategy section of the book.

Yes, it will take a while. But these articles will move up in the search results rather quickly for their specific keyword.

*Every morning, check your web page's ranking for your keywords in SEMrush.* **Keep in mind, keyword position tracking can be volatile day-by-day.**

One day you're ranking in position 50, the next you're ranking in position 2. Then a week later you're in position 20. The longer your content is on the internet, the more stable your ranking position will become.

*So give it about a month to stabilize before making radical changes.*

## Congratulations!

You have completed the content strategy for your article. Rinse and repeat for all of the other keywords on your list.

# YouTube Video Strategy
## How to Double-Rank Your Content with YouTube

In the 2017 version of this book, I had the YouTube strategy as a "bonus" section. But now, it's absolutely necessary if you want to stand a chance at ranking highly in 2018.

**You don't have a choice anymore.**

You need to get on the video train or you'll be left in the dust at the station, my friend. *It's estimated that by 2020 almost 80% of online traffic will be for video… that's only two years away!*

The amount of time people spend on YouTube is up over 60% from last year and 55% of all Google search results contain at least one video.

## Dwell Time & Rankbrain

As if any of the aforementioned details are not inspiring enough, let me tell you about Google's Rankbrain and the dwell time factor. Unlike, Google Panda and Penguin updates, *Rankbrain is not a classic mathematical computer algorithm.*

Rankbrain is an interpretation model with underlying artificial intelligence and machine learning capabilities. It's one of the main pieces of technology helping Google sort search results today.

It measures how users interact with search results, noting where they click and how long they spend on a web page.

**The amount of time a user spends on a web page after posing a query is called "dwell time" and it's becoming one of the leading factors in ranking on the first page.**

**For top 10 Google search results, the average dwell time is 3 minutes and 10 seconds.**

So if a user is spending less than 3 minutes on your content, *you will likely never see your search result on the first page of Google.*

It's a harsh reality, but a surefire way to compete is by coupling your written content with a 15 minute YouTube video.

You are much more likely to have users stick around for 3 minutes watching an engaging video than reading a text-only article. *Our society's attention span is shortening, and reading text is becoming lackluster due to all the competing visual images and videos.*

Google is in the information business and strives to give users the fastest, most efficient, and most complete answer first. They want someone to find the answer they are looking for without having to jump around to different websites.

**That's why it's so important to cover entire topics in depth.**

When you endeavor to cover an entire subject in depth, it should be fairly easy to create a 15-minute long video about it.

The best part? *Almost everyone is too lazy to get involved with video, no matter how strongly you communicate the need to them.* So take advantage of it and get ahead fast! This section will guide you through the YouTube ranking process.

When users search directly on YouTube, they will see videos presented in a similar manner ranking-wise as a regular Google search query.

However, when users search on Google, if a relevant video features the same keywords and answers the question, *Google will rank the YouTube video in regular Google search results along with web page results.*

**This allows you to rank both a web page AND a YouTube video on the first page of Google.** Videos may be hard and time consuming, but it's totally worth it. I've had massive success with double-ranking content using YouTube videos in tandem with web page/article content.

More recently in the past few months, YouTube videos are ranking in image results as well. *There are so many great opportunities with video content using YouTube, so let's get to it.*

**Here's an overview of what you will learn, step-by-step, in this section and the estimated time it will take you to complete each task:**

- ☐ Create a Video (2-6 Hrs)
- ☐ Create a Thumbnail (30 Min)
- ☐ Text, Titles, CC, & Descriptions (30 Min)
- ☐ Generate Embed Video Code (5 Min)

# Create Your YouTube Video

Good news: most of the work has already been done for you (by you.) Using the prioritized keyword list you originally created for articles, you are going to create video versions.

**Remember to create the videos based on priority determined by search volume on your prioritized keyword list.**

The content you already created for each keyword can be used as an aid to create the script for your video.

When writing the video script, consider how YouTube determines quality and relevance of a video ranking-wise.

## User Experience Factors

User experience on YouTube is calculated based on a myriad of variables. A few of these variables that will determine your video's ranking include:

- How many positive comments your video generates
- How many "thumbs up" your video receives
- How long viewers watch your video
- How many people subscribe to your channel after watching your video
- How many viewers "favorite" your video
- How many people share your video via social media

Make your video interesting and engaging. **Remember that reading content is vastly different from watching and listening to content.** *When using your article to create a script, factor in visual aids, voice inflection, and how speaking to someone differs from writing to someone.*

I suggest typing some of your keywords into YouTube and watching the first few videos that show up. **Generate ideas on how to make your content more engaging and informative than the competition.**

Also, read the comments for the videos. Consider the negative comments and figure out how you can make your video better. **Remember to outsource if you get stuck.**

## Short Summary & Hooks

Create a short summary of the video's main points to place at the beginning of the video. That way, when viewers start to watch your video, they will know what is in store.

Typically, you want to give them enough information to orient them on what your video will cover, **while simultaneously piquing their interest to encourage them to keep watching the video until the very end.**

Just like in the content creation section earlier in the book, you want to lace the video with hooks to keep viewers watching.

Here's a sample list of hooks you can use throughout the video to keep your viewers watching:

- Here's the Deal
- But Here's the Kicker
- Here's the Bottom Line
- Want to Know the Best Part?
- That's Not All
- What's the Catch?
- Listen to This
- The Truth Is

## 10+ Minute Video Length

Similar to creating written content that is at least 2K words in length, the gold standard for YouTube video length that ranks well is at least 10 minutes. In fact, most videos ranking on the first page of search results are an average of 15 minutes long now.

Once you've written your script, *I suggest you time yourself while reading the content out loud in a manner you intend to record it.* This will help you determine whether or not the script is long enough to create a 10+ minute video.

**If your video is at the appropriate length of at least 10 minutes, then you are ready to move on.** If it's short of the 10 minute mark, keep adding more informative and high-quality content until you're there.

## Video File Name

Once your video is finished, rename the video's filename to your video's keyword. For example, if your video's keyword is "how to play the organ," then name the image file "how_to_play_the_organ.mp4"

**This is a crucial step. Make sure the video's filename is the same as the video's keyword BEFORE uploading it.**

# Create a Thumbnail

Thumbnails on YouTube are the still pictures shown when the video appears in search results. While not necessarily a ranking factor, **it does dictate whether or not people are inspired to click on your video to watch it.**

Just like the featured image of an article, **a unique, high-quality thumbnail is statistically more likely to get clicked on than a video with a default one.** *When more people choose to click on your video, more people watch your video, and it's more likely to rise up in rankings.*

You can create a unique, high-quality image in a number of ways:

- Take your own photographs
- Hire a photographer to take photographs for you
- Find images online and make them unique via Photoshop
- Hire someone on Upwork to create unique images for you
- Try Visme, it's a free visual image creator with YouTube thumbnail templates

Once the unique, high-quality, relevant image has been created, **rename the image's filename to your video's keyword.** For example, if your video's keyword is "how to start a business," then name the image file "how to start a business.jpg"

Set the image as the thumbnail of the video during the upload process.

# Title, CC, & Descriptions

These are all the variables you will add during the upload process.

## Video Title

This is the easy part. Your title is already done. Use the same title as the corresponding keyword article: complete with brackets, parenthesis, and keywords.

## Closed Captioning

Using the script you created the video with, add it to the video in the form of closed captioning. **This is how YouTube and Google know what words are coming out of your mouth.** *This is also why it's important not to use your article verbatim as a script because you run the risk of creating duplicate content.*

The process is very easy and Google has a great step-by-step guide on how to do it here.

## Video Description

This is one of the most important ranking variables for YouTube videos: descriptions. Similar to closed captioning, since YouTube and Google can't understand what you say throughout the video (yet), they rely heavily on the text in the description.

**In the first line of the description, include a link to your website.** This will function as a backlink and will increase your website's click-through rate.

**Next, make sure you use your video's keyword at least once in the first 30 words of the description.**

**Then ensure the entire description is at least 300 words in length. Also, make sure the video's keyword is used between 2 to 4 times throughout the description.** I suggest using the summary you created for the beginning of the video as a basis for the description.

That way, all the video's content points are covered in the description if a viewer decides to read the description before watching your video.

## Tags

The final section of the upload includes a section for "tags." Add tags using your keywords, LSI keywords, synonyms, or other variations of the keyword. Also consider adding the names of your competitors YouTube channels as tags. This will increase your likelihood of showing up for results when people type in their names.

# Generate Video Embed Code

Once your video is uploaded to YouTube, you need to embed it into the corresponding content page on your website. **The best way to ensure the video is shareable and can easily create backlinks for you is by generating a video embed code.**

## Embed Code Generator

Here is a link to a free embed code generator: https://www.siegemedia.com/embed-code-generator. Follow the link, choose the "Embed Video" tab, and simply fill in all of the blank fields with the appropriate data.

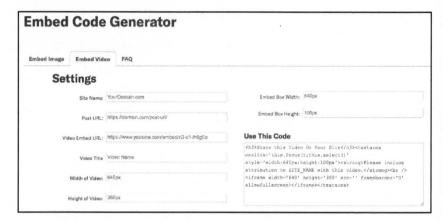

Once you've generated the embed code, use it to place the video into your web page. This embed code will make it extremely easy for users to share your video and create backlinks to your content.

## Congratulations!

You have completed the YouTube strategy for your double-ranking efforts. Rinse and repeat for all of the other keywords on your list.

# Add Structured-Data Mark-up

## What is Structured-Data Markup?

Now that you've created a content masterpiece, it's time to make Google's job easier when featuring your content in search results. You can achieve this through structured-data markup.

Structured data is a standardized format Google uses to classify aspects of web pages. **It's basically Google's own personal filing system for indexing webpages more quickly and easily.**

In action, structured-data markup will communicate to Google if a web page features an event versus a cooking recipe. Both are treated differently to increase the user's experience when conducting a search.

## Why Add Structured-Data Markup?

Depending on the content type, *Google Search will display rich sets of features for your page when you provide them with structured data markup.*

So an event will show dates, ticket pricing, and other relevant details in a clean format. While a cooking recipe will likely show up in a carousel format that allows the user to swipe through relevant recipes featuring pictures, reviews, and instructions.

These search features vary widely depending on location, the device type, and the ever-changing algorithms behind the scenes collecting data and deciding which page to display for search results.

**And remember, Google is always testing and adopting tactics that lead to faster, more high-quality results for its users.**

Google is obviously having success with featured snippets, so if you want your content to stand a chance at displaying on the first page for a search query, your content needs to be riddled with structured-data markup.

## Search Feature Enhancements

Here are a few types of features, or "search enhancements", Google may use to display your page when you employ structured data markup:

Breadcrumbs

Breadcrumbs, or breadcrumb trails, show where a page in a search result resides in the overall hierarchy of the website. This feature is used to categorize content and allow users to quickly understand where the content is located in relation to the main website for navigation in mobile searches.

Here is an example of breadcrumbs displayed in a Google search query for "winter books":

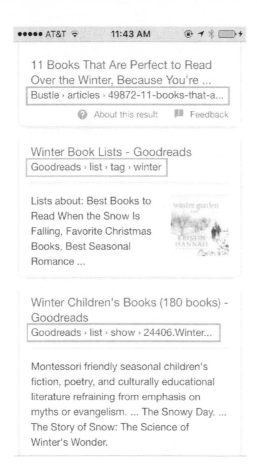

Notice how it acts as a secondary form of navigation, displaying the main website to the left followed by a succession of narrowing categories: "Goodreads > list > tag > winter"

Sitelinks Searchbox

This feature helps users do more in-depth searches on a particular website when they perform a search. In the search results, a separate search box will appear that allows the user to conduct a search for content within that specific website.

For example, if you perform a search for "Zillow," you will see the sitelinks searchbox in action:

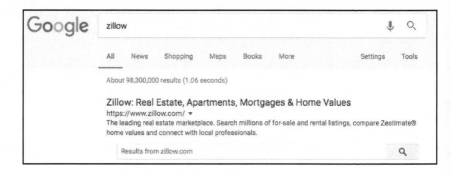

## Corporate Contacts

When a user searches for a corporation, this feature will prominently display the contact information for the business. *Using this type of structured data markup on your company's website will add your business' information to Google's knowledge panels.*

Here is an example of the corporate contacts feature in a Google knowledge panel for search results:

## Logos

Similar to the corporate contacts feature, when you use structured data markup to identify your company's logo, it will prominently display on Google's knowledge panel.

Here is an example of a business' logo shown on a knowledge panel:

# MakerBot

3D printing company

 makerbot.com

MakerBot is an American desktop 3D printer manufacturer company headquartered in New York City. It was founded in January 2009 by Bre Pettis, Adam Mayer, and Zach "Hoeken" Smith to MakerBot build on the early progress of the RepRap Project. Wikipedia

**Founded:** January 2009

**CEO:** Jonathan Jaglom (Mar 1, 2015-)

**Headquarters:** New York City, NY

**Founders:** Bre Pettis, Adam Mayer, Zach "Hoeken" Smith

**Parent organization:** Stratasys

## Social Profile Links

In addition to corporate contacts and logos, Google will also display any social media links provided in the structured data markup for your website in the knowledge panels. It's quick and easy for a user to access on the fly.

Here is an example of social profile links on knowledge panels:

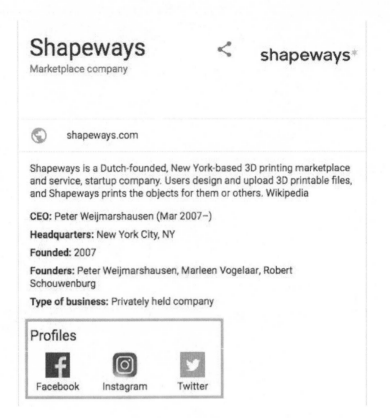

## Carousels

One of the more unique search features is called carousels. These are primarily displayed for mobile search results.

Carousels can be used to display list-like formats of similar content. **The format allows users to swipe through relevant content featuring pictures, reviews, and summaries.**

Google has reported that certain types of content will automatically display in a carousel format without the use of structured markup data. The types of content likely to be featured in a carousel include recipes, films, and articles.

Here is an example of a carousel for a recipe query:

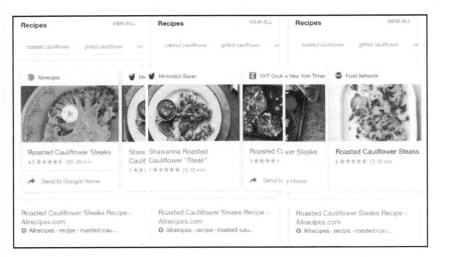

# Qualifying Content Types

Below is a list of the content types that qualify to display in an enhanced search format. Each type is a hyperlink that takes you to Google's Search Guide for that particular type of content.

- Articles

- Books

- Courses

- Datasets

- Events

- Fact Check

- Job Postings

- Local Businesses

- Music

- Paywalled Content

- Podcasts

- Products

- Recipes

- Reviews

- TV & Movies

- Videos

# How to Add Structured-Data Mark-up:

Here are the step-by-step instructions on how to add structured-data markup to your content.

**Step 1:** Sign in to your Google Search Console account by going to this link:

https://www.google.com/webmasters/tools/

Once you are signed in, you will reach a screen that looks something like this:

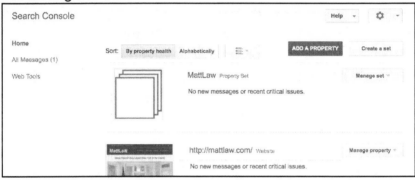

**Step 2:** Choose the Google Property linked to your website and under "Search Appearance," select "Data Highlighter."

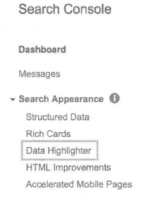

**Step 3:** The next screen will look similar to the one below. Click on the "Start Highlighting" button.

**Step 4:** A window will appear requesting the following: the URL to the content, the content type from a dropdown, and a radio button asking if you want to markup just one page or all other similar pages. Once you've made the proper selections, click "OK."

In the following example, we will markup a local business page.

Enter the URL of a typical page on your site

https://southtampapaintball.com

Local Businesses

○ Tag this page and others like it
● Tag just this page

OK    Close

**Step 5:** The next screen should display your page on the left and a blank information panel on the right. Within your web page displayed on the left, use your mouse to click and highlight pertinent information, such as telephone numbers.

As you click and drag your mouse over the information, the text will highlight and a dropdown of information types will appear.

If you highlighted a phone number, select "Telephone" from the dropdown like in the example below:

If there is an address on the page, highlight that and select "Address":

If the business name appears, highlight it and select "Name":

day! South Tampa Paintball

who wishes to Play Paintbal

ps of 14 or more Players.

If your hours of operation are listed, highlight it and select "Operating hours":

# OPEN SATURDAYS & SUNDAYS 10AM-5PM

*(813) 775-7110*

**Step 6:** Review the choices in the dropdown field and ensure any corresponding information displayed on your web page has been highlighted. Once everything has been highlighted, click on the "Publish" button in the top right-hand corner.

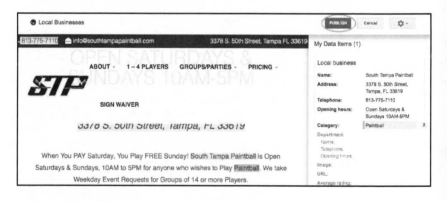

**Step 7:** Next, you will be brought back to a screen similar to the one below. This is where you can review your data highlighter submission:

Click the "Start Highlighting" button and repeat steps 4 through 6 until all of your content has structured-data mark-up!

**Step 8:** Keep up to date with the latest Google Search Features and Structured Data Guidelines with Google's comprehensive online guide here: https://developers.google.com/search/docs/guides/

Note from Google on Structured Data:

Even though you have marked up your content with structured data, Google does not guarantee it will show up in search results. See Google's note below:

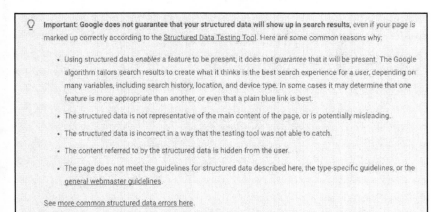

Here are the links within the notice you can reference:

- <u>Structured Data Testing Tool</u>
- <u>General Webmaster Guidelines</u>
- <u>More Common Structured Data Errors Here</u>

## Congratulations!

You have completed structured-data markup for your article. Rinse and repeat for all of the other pages on your website.

# Linking Strategy

Now that your content is optimized for success, it's time to sit back and watch it percolate to the top of Google's search results, right?

*Wrong.*

*Google asserts that the # 1 and # 2 ranking factors are content and LINKS.* You need to promote your content and share it with the world to **build credibility and authority.**

Most content ranking on the first page of Google have a lot of high-quality sites linking to that specific piece of content. *When other websites link to a piece of your content, that generates a backlink for you.*

The more websites that link to a piece of content, the more high-quality the content tends to be, hence its importance in determining page rank.

More recently, it's become less about the *amount* of back-links and **more about the quality of those backlinks.**

A website with a high page authority in Google's eyes will create a higher quality backlink. For example, if Forbes or the Wall Street Journal linked to a piece of your content, *their backlink is weighed considerably more than another lesser known website.* A backlink from WSJ would increase your ranking potential immensely.

**Building backlinks is paramount to succeeding in SEO. It's challenging and it's time-consuming.** However, once your content gains some momentum, it will be worth it.

Proper execution of the backlink strategy in this section will boost your content's ranking in Google's search results.

You do not need to necessarily adopt *every single strategy in this backlink section for every single piece of content you create*, but adopting a few of them will improve your ranking over time.

**Here's an overview of what you will learn, step-by-step, in this section and the estimated time it will take you to complete each task:**

- ☐ Create List of High-Authority, Niche-Relevant Websites (30 Min)
- ☐ Create Cornerstone Content (Days, Weeks, or Months)
- ☐ Conduct & Publish Interviews (4 to 6 Hrs)
- ☐ Write Reviews, Comparisons, or Testimonials (2 to 4 Hrs)
- ☐ Promote Your Content (30 Min per Article)
- ☐ External Linking (10-20 Min per Article)
- ☐ Q&A Websites (5-20 Min per Question)
- ☐ HARO (10-20 Min per Opportunity)
- ☐ Scholarship Offer (1 Hr One-time Setup)
- ☐ Infographics (1 Hr per Infographic)
- ☐ Toxic Link Removal (5-10 Min)

# Create List of High Quality Niche Relevant Websites

**The primary goal of this section is to get an editorially placed link to your content in a good position on high-authority, niche-relevant websites.** First, you need to seek out and approach the best websites for your backlinking strategy.

There are four variables to create a perfect backlink: the website domain should have high authority, the website should jive with your niche, the link must be editorially placed, and the link must be embedded in a good position on the page.

*These are the four variables you will use to create a list of high-authority, niche-relevant websites:*

1. **High-Authority Websites**
    a. A link from a high authority website like Huffington Post will pack more of a positive backlink punch than a random blog site. Go to <u>Ahrefs</u>, put in a URL, and check out its URL Rating and Domain Rating to determine the website's authority. (UR = URL Rating and DR = Domain Rating)

**UR** <sup>i</sup>
**34**

**DR** <sup>i</sup>
**42**

2. **Niche-Relevant Websites**
    a. You need backlinks from similarly categorized websites. For example, if your website is about gardening, then backlinks from a car repair website will not help you. Aim for authoritative websites that have some sort of relevance with your content and theme.
3. **Editorially Placed Link**
    a. This is when someone posts a link to your website *because they genuinely liked your content*, as opposed to a random website that randomly creates links to places. Google is smart enough to determine the contextual relationship between websites, links, and content, so editorially placed links foster much more ranking weight than random ones.
4. **Good Link Position**
    a. A link to your website on the side or footer of

a page is worth significantly less than a link within the body of the page's content. *When your link is embedded in the middle of another page's content, you will reap the benefits of backlinking.* Always aim to have your content linked in the middle of the another page's content, not tucked away at the bottom or in a sidebar.

Once you've created a comprehensive list of websites, you need to figure out the best way to pitch or promote your content to them in order to secure a sweet backlink in a good position on their page.

# Create Cornerstone Content

Original data and research is a backlink goldmine.

Think about it.

Most of the interesting content on the internet is rife with interesting facts and data from other sources.

**So why not BECOME that source of data and information people use to generate content?**

This is one of the most challenging and most rewarding ways to secure backlinks. *It's extremely time-consuming and can take days, weeks, or months depending on the type of data you're collecting.*

However, once you create it, you can earn backlinks from anyone who references your data in a blog, video, infographic, social media post, or anything! People can use your findings to create a whole bunch of new content. *The possibilities are endless.*

The best way to go about creating cornerstone content people can reference is as follows:

1. **Conduct Research to Gather Data**
    a. Choose a narrow scope to analyze on a topic relevant to your niche. The more representative and relevant your research is to your niche, the more valuable it will be to content generators.
        i. **Experiments** - If you are into gardening, you could decide to conduct an experiment using different types of grow lights on cucumber seedlings for 60 days.
        ii. **Research Papers** - If you are a political enthusiast, you could gather facts and information from scholarly articles or historical documents to create a research paper about the formation and evolution of the Icelandic government.
        iii. **Surveys** - If you are a psychologist specializing in anxiety, you can have your patient's fill out surveys for a few months to gather data to share with the world.
        iv. **Case Studies** - If you are a drum teacher, you could use different teaching techniques with different students and keep track of their progress for data.
2. **Organize and Publish Data**
    a. Organize the data in a way that is easy to digest and *create visual media such as graphs, charts, and other helpful designs to lace throughout the publication.*
    b. Publish the data.
3. **Create Content Using Your Cornerstone Piece**
    a. You can use your own data to create a series of videos, blogs, newsletters, or the like. This is a great way to generate fresh content and to promote your research.
4. **Promote Your Cornerstone Content**
    a. If you completed step one sufficiently, the

audience within your niche will likely be very receptive to an email or message sharing your article.

b. You can skip down to the "Promote Your Content" section for more ideas on how to secure a backlink through promotion.

# Conduct & Publish Interviews

Similar to cornerstone content, your audience would love to consume information from an interview of a leader or highly experienced person in your niche. *Interviews are highly shareable forms of content that will create great backlinks for your content.*

**A successful interview is comprised of two things:**
1. **The right person**
2. **The right questions**

Be highly selective in who you choose to interview. Industry leaders and influencers who are well known within your niche will work best.

The right questions will also make or break your interview. Your audience will be most interested in learning about best practices in their industry, how the interviewee has realized success in the niche, and other valuable types of information.

Follow these steps to create a highly shareable interview:

1. **Research, Research, Research**
   a. Figure out what your audience deems valuable and find the right influencer to interview for information.
2. **Prepare Your Questions**
   a. Create a list of the most important questions your audience would likely want to learn about.

Your questions should spark their curiosity and the answers should satiate your audience.

3. **Stay Open to Tangents**
   a. Scripted interviews do not work as well as ones that flow naturally. Always be prepared to keep your interviewee on track, but also give them some slack to explore other things that are interesting. Ask followup questions your audience may find helpful as well.

4. **Organize and Publish the Interview**
   a. Organize the interview in a way that is easy to digest and *create visual media such as graphs, quotes, and other helpful designs to lace throughout the publication.*
   b. Publish the interview.

5. **Promote Your Interview**
   a. If you completed step one sufficiently, the audience within your niche will likely be very receptive to an email or message sharing your interview.
   b. You can skip down to the "Promote Your Content" section for more ideas on how to secure a backlink through promotion.

# Write Reviews, Comparisons, or Testimonials

Reviews, comparisons, or testimonials of products, services, techniques, events, or just about anything related to your niche *are highly shareable forms of media when done well.*

People find personal opinions interesting and valuable, especially if you have a lot of knowledge on a subject or have been in the field a long time.

If you are in the travel niche, you know there are a ton of great, high-quality sites out there teeming with amazing information. *Backlinks from these sites would propel you to the top of search results rather easily.*

Choosing a topic to write a review or comparison about is key. **You need to pick something fresh and unique to catch their attention.**

Imagine you've visited a lot of vineyards and wineries in Thailand and had enough knowledge to write an amazing review or comparison. Creating content like this could be easily picked up by travel sites that focus on the south east Asia region or Thailand specifically.

Or imagine you are into gardening and you've tried out a few different types of seedling soil to grow broccoli. *An in-depth review or comparison of the soils would be an attractive article to feature on authority gardening sites.*

**Get creative and stick with what you know within your niche.** People are always searching for specific solutions or information for their specific problems or situations.

Generate a list of ideas to write reviews or comparisons about, follow the steps in the content creation section to optimize it, and then promote the content by emailing the web managers of some websites from your niche site list.

Depending on the nature of your review, the business associated with the product, service, or event would likely be receptive to featuring your review on their website, creating an awesome backlink for you!

You can skip down to the "Promote Your Content" section for more ideas on how to secure a backlink through promotion.

# Promote Your Content

Promoting your content is crucial to developing backlinks. Below are a some link building strategies you can implement to pitch your content.

# Get Listed on Resource Pages

Resource pages list links to content regarding a specific topic. Finding a resource page that could potentially list your content is simple using Google search.

**Simply search for your keyword in quotes, followed by + inurl:links.** For example, the search query "gardening" + inurl:links revealed several results for gardening resource pages.

When you find some potential pages, check the website's URL and domain ranking using Ahrefs, then determine whether or not your content would be a good fit.

If everything checks out, locate an email address to contact the person who manages the website's content.

*Draft a personalized email promoting your content.* Here is an example of how you can structure your email to send out to resource pages:

> "Greetings, Travel Happy!

> As I was searching for Asia travel tips earlier today, I stumbled upon your resource page listing several interesting links about travelling in Asia: https://travel-happy.info/travel-links/asia-travel-links-roundup/

> Your link to the Khao Yai winery was particularly exciting! I too have grown very fond of Thai wine. Thank you so much for featuring it on the resource page.

> Interestingly enough, I recently posted a guide on Thai wine. It's about my experience travelling in Thailand and visiting wineries around the country.

You should check it out if you have the chance: example.com/thai-wine-travels

Let me know what you think. If you enjoy the guide, maybe it might be a nice fit for your resource page? Either way, thank you so much for sharing your resource page. I look forward to checking out Khao Yai in the future.

Thanks for your time and have an awesome day!"

**It's important to make the email as personalized as possible to increase your chances of earning a backlink.**

Generate a list of potential resource pages, start drafting some emails, and wait for the backlinks to start flowing. *Remember, maintain momentum!* Always keep an eye out for more resource link opportunities.

## Replace Broken Links

Over time, some of the external links featured within great content break. Either a website moved, the URL changed, or it simply doesn't exist anymore. Using a free Chrome plugin called LinkMiner, **you can quickly locate broken links on any page within the Chrome browser.**

You can conduct Google searches for relevant content and run LinkMiner to try to find broken links your content could potentially replace. Remember to always check the website's URL and domain ranking using Ahrefs when scouring the web for backlink providers.

Once you find a high-quality, niche-relevant website with broken links, draft an email to promote your content. You can say something like:

"Greetings, Travel Happy!

As I was searching for Asia travel tips earlier today, I stumbled upon your resource page listing several interesting links about travelling in Asia: https://travel-happy.info/travel-links/asia-travel-links-roundup/

Unfortunately, a few links about Thai wine aren't working right:

Example1.com
Example2.com

Interestingly enough, I just posted a guide about Thai wine a few months ago. You can check it out here: example.com/thai-wine-travels

Let me know if you like it. I think it could be a good replacement for the broken links. Thank you for sharing your page, I greatly enjoyed it. Hopefully this helped you out.

Thanks for your time and have a great day!"

As previously stated, **make sure your emails are as personalized as possible to increase your chances of receiving a response… and hopefully a backlink!**

## Pre-Publish Outreach

Before you publish some of your content, try some pre-publish outreach. Let's say you created a definitive guide to Thai winery travel. Using the list of websites you created earlier, pinpoint the ones that your content would benefit the most.

Draft an email to each individual website and pitch your content. Your email can read something like this:

"Greetings, Travel Happy!

I've been following your blog for a year or so now. I really love your content about Thailand. It's helped me out immensely during my travels there.

I was wondering if you had any upcoming Thailand articles in the works? I've been working hard on a definitive guide to Thai wineries that I think would be a great fit for your website.

It features travel tips and in-depth information about each winery, including history, wine-making processes, and suggestions about where to lodge.

Let me know if this sounds like something you would be interested in featuring. Thank you again for sharing such great content. I truly love reading your stuff. Thanks again and have a great day!"

**Another approach to pre-publish outreach includes sending emails to any brands, products, services, or businesses you mention throughout your post.** Using the Thai winery example, you could draft an email to send to each winery or lodging recommendation you make.

Or if your article includes any links to an external blog, you can email them as well. Send a link to your post to any website that responds positively to the pre-publish outreach email.

If they think it's a good fit, *then you will harness some great backlinks upon publication of your post.*

# External Linking

## What is External Linking?

External links refer to any hyperlinks that link to another website or domain different from your own. Remember earlier we talked about internal links, which linked content that existed on your website to other content on your same website?

Well, this is the same concept, except you are linking to content on different websites. **Hopefully after completing the entire backlink strategy section of this book, other high-quality, authority websites will host external links on their website that lead to your content.**

## Why is External Linking Important?

External linking has been proven to increase content ranking. *Some even believe external links are the most powerful source of rank strength.*

This is because search engines, like Google, treat links to your website from other websites as them sort of "vouching" for the validity and quality of your content.

So, Google perceives other websites linking to your content as them "liking" your content. Google is all about delivering high-quality, relevant content to searchers, so **Google takes external links into serious consideration when evaluating the rank-worthiness of your content.**

Conversely, when you include external links from your website to another authoritative website with relevant content, *it will also positively affect your ranking.* In this particular section, we will discuss how to properly link to external content.

In later sections of this book, we will describe how to secure external links that point to your website from authoritative sources.

# How to Add External Links to Your Content:

**Step 1:** Figure out what relevant content, media, or graphic would add value to your existing article. Relevance is crucial! Do not include external links that do not naturally flow from your article to the external content.

**The natural flow of the information is extremely critical.**

For example, if your article is about "how to find a job after law school," and in the first paragraph you discuss how the legal market is saturated, perhaps a chart or graph depicting the phenomena would be good to include. Then you would want to find an accurate, relevant chart that is from a credible, reliable, and authoritative source.

Another example would be if your keyword was "how to teach your dog tricks," and you discuss the use of treats for training. You could link to an article that lists different types of healthy treats for dogs.

An additional example: if your keyword is "how to paint with watercolors," you may want to includes photos with external links to watercolor artwork. Or, if your opening paragraph briefly mentions the origins of watercoloring, then you can add an external link to an article about a detailed history of watercolor art.

**Step 2:** Find an authoritative website or source for the external content you want to add to your article.

This can be as complex of a process as you want. But the two easiest, most sure-fire ways to locate an authoritative website are as follows:

- Type in keywords related to the content you want to add and make a list of all of the websites that are on the first couple pages of Google's search results.
- Go to Ahrefs, put in a URL, and check out its URL Rating and Domain Rating

Search engines like Google take into consideration things like the trustworthiness, popularity, relevance, and relationship between the external links. **Make sure it's a website you want to associate with your website.**

*Try to keep the sources you use relevant to your market or industry.* For example, if you are in real estate, try to associate with websites that are in your industry. That way, Google always knows your niche.

**Step 3:** Create a hyperlink to the other website's content within your article. Remember, as we discussed in the "internal links" section of Content Strategy: it helps your ranking to use keywords in the link text, *HOWEVER, it's risky to use keywords every single time.*

Many scammy websites use keywords to link to external content. So, frequent use of keywords in link text is a red flag. No more than 10-20% of the links should include exact or partial keywords. Use brand names or more natural linking terms for the rest of the domains.

I recommend hyperlinking what sounds most natural. Sometimes it might be, "click here to read more." Or it might be, "for more information, check out this guide about how to choose the best dog treats." Or it might be, "use dog treats throughout the training process."

**Again, be careful and always do what's natural.**

Creating a link to external content is extremely easy on WordPress:

- First, highlight the text you wish to make a hyperlink.
- Then, scroll up to the WordPress Editor and click the chainlink graphic on the toolbar like this:

- Next, paste the link to the external content into the text field and click on the blue arrow to finish the linking process.

**Step 4:** Repeat Steps 1 through 3 for each article you want to insert external links within. **Try to aim for an average of 3 outbound external links per 1,000 words throughout the article for optimal performance.**

# Q&A Websites

## What are Q&A Websites?

Question and answer, or Q&A, websites are online communities where users pose questions that other users can answer. Examples of these types of websites include Quora, Yahoo Answers, WikiHow, Amazon's Askville, and Answers. com.

## Why Should You Register to Q&A Websites?

Registering to high-quality Q&A websites like Quora will allow you to answer questions about topics relevant to your website or blog. Since Quora is an authoritative web source, when people type questions into Google that have been answered on Quora, they will often be featured on the first page of Google.

If you happened to give the best, high-quality answer, when web searchers read the Quora post, *they will be exposed to your answer to the posed question.* Over time, if done correctly, **you will be viewed as a reliable expert on your specific topic.**

By following the steps below, you can also increase your own website's ranking while answering questions on sites like Quora.

## How to Use Q&A Websites:

**Step 1:** Register to Q&A websites. I recommend starting out with Quora and registering through your Google+ account. That way, Google trusts your authorship and the information you provide on Quora.

**Step 2:** Add any information to your user profile that didn't get populated from your Google+ account. Make sure you have a professional profile picture that people can trust. Create a clear, concise description of the type of work you do and your expertise.

Creating a high-quality user profile will give you credibility and authority from the users' and Q&A site's perspective. You will come off as a trustworthy and reliable source of information.

**Step 3:** For the first 30 days, focus on answering questions posed by other Quora users about things relevant to your website's content and your expertise. *DO NOT link back to your website (yet!)*

**Only focus on crafting well-thought-out, high-quality, answers to the questions.**

Just like the content creation strategy: you want to write the best answer to these people's questions. After a day or so, you will notice other Quora users will start to request your answers to their related questions.

Sign in to the Q&A site every day and provide extensive, easy-to-understand answers to other users' questions. After 30 days, you should have received some upvotes on the answers you provided and people will have started to take notice of your expertise in your niche.

Share your answers on your social media channels. Quora makes it easy to do.

**Step 4:** After 30 days have passed, slowly and cautiously start including links to any relevant content you have on your website about the question at hand. For example, if someone asks a simple question about 401(k) plans, answer the question to the best of your ability, still ensuring a high-quality answer.

Then, casually and naturally mention, "If you would like to read a more in-depth guide about 401(k) plans you can check out my Guide to 401(k) plans by clicking here. Please let me know if you need any additional information."

Remember, do this *only when your website's content is absolutely relevant to the question and can naturally flow with your answer.* **Be smart and cautious when building backlinks to your website from Q&A websites.** Take it slow and easy. Don't overdo it.

**Step 5:** If you see the same or similar questions frequently arise on your topic of expertise, consider keeping track of the questions you encounter and creating an article about it on your website.

**Step 6:** Keep answering questions and keep your answers high-quality. Eventually you will be viewed as an expert on your subject, and the slow, progressive backlinks from these authoritative Q&A websites **will increase the authority of your own website.** The byproduct of this, of course, is an increase in search rankings.

Pro-Tip: Repeat steps 1 through 6 for "expert forums."

On the internet, there are some forums that are dedicated to certain niches or specialties. Make sure you read the rules of each forum carefully before proceeding. *Some forums prohibit the use of links or require anonymity with user profiles.*

Spend your time wisely. Look at the latest post of a forum. If no recent posts exist within the past week or month, it's likely a slow, dead forum that won't be worth your time. **Only spend time on high-quality, active, authoritative forums.**

# HARO

## What is HARO?

HARO stands for "Help a Reporter Out." It's the name of a website. The URL is https://www.helpareporter.com. This website is a place where journalists from prestigious news companies go to find sources for upcoming stories they want to publish.

## Why Use HARO?

HARO is used by journalists who publish articles, stories, and media to big-time news agencies like Fox News, the Chicago Tribune, TIME Magazine, The New York Times, WSJ, and ABC.

When you sign up with HARO as an expert source of information, you add yourself to a data pool where journalists are searching for *someone like you to quote or use in an article that will be published on a high-quality, authoritative, news media website.*

If selected as a source, **you can gain extremely high-quality external links from an authority news agency like WSJ to your website directly.** HUGE!

## How to Use HARO:

**Step 1:** Read the "Rules for Sources" page on HARO here: https://www.helpareporter.com/sources/rules/ Make sure you follow the rules to stay a part of the community. You don't want to get kicked off and lose such a valuable opportunity to secure powerful external links to your website from news sources.

**Step 2:** Sign up for HARO as a source here: https://www.helpareporter.com/subscriptions/basic/

**Step 3:** Choose to be a source for the categories that most closely relate to your expertise.

**Step 4:** Check your daily HARO emails as soon as they arrive. The emails usually include a list of thirty or so topics reporters are looking for information about, and **they often need the information from prospective sources in less than 48 hours.**

It is crucial to read the HARO emails as soon as they arrive to figure out if any of the queries are relevant to your particular expertise.

**Step 5:** Respond to the reports *ASAP.* Again, once you find a topic that you can respond to, **respond as soon as possible in a high-quality fashion.**

**Step 6:** Repeat steps 4 and 5 until you are chosen to be featured as an expert or source of information.

**Step 7:** Make sure the reporter or journalist has a link to your website or relevant article to include in their news piece.

**Step 8:** Share the article you were featured in on your social media outlets.

**Step 9:** Once you start building a repertoire of great news articles you were featured in as an expert, consider creating an "In the News" section on your website where you can put all the links to the news articles you contributed to.

## Pro-Tip: Search for Guest-Blogging Opportunities

Type your keyword into Google search with "guest post," "submit guest blog," or "guest author," and try to find a high-quality or authoritative website that is accepting guest blog posts on your topic. Use Twitter to try to find some opportunities as well.

If you find one, write an article the same way described in the content strategy section, bearing in mind the article will go on another website.

**When your guest blog post is published, it will create yet another powerful external link to your website.**

Once your website or blog becomes a big-timer, you may consider opening up a spot for a guest blogger. This will also create powerful backlinks to your website from the guest's blogs.

Caution: Note on Guest Blogging

Recently, Google warned web publishers that heavily rely on guest posting for link building about increased scrutinization of their sites in an effort to minimize the proliferation of spammy links.

Avoid websites that rely solely on guest blogging for content, websites unrelated to your niche, and websites that pay guests to publish posts.

So, be mindful of this when entertaining the idea of guest blogging and be highly selective to protect the integrity of your website's backlinks.

# Scholarship Offer

## What is a Scholarship Offer?

A scholarship offer is exactly what you think it is: offer a monetary scholarship to college students. What? Why?

## Why Create a Scholarship Offer?

One of the most powerful types of external links come from .edu websites. When a website ends is ".edu" it indicates the website represents an academic organization. So it's real, credible, and authoritative.

**Google trusts .edu websites, therefore, they are great backlink sources.**

Almost every single college has a section or page of their website dedicated to scholarship opportunities for their students. When you offer a scholarship to college students, *you are eligible to have your scholarship page linked to the .edu website's scholarship pages.*

**The byproduct of that is an incredibly powerful backlink that will undoubtedly have a positive effect on your ranking.** Also, it's charitable and tax-deductible!

## How to Create a Scholarship Offer:

**Step 1:** Create a page on your website totally dedicated to your scholarship offer. On the page, outline the application process.

For example, if you are a financial advisor trying to increase the rank of your website and decide to offer a scholarship, the offer on your web page can look something like this:

*Downtown NYC Investing LLC Quarterly $500 Scholarships*

Our financial advising team at Downtown NYC Investing LLC believes in supporting student's dreams by offering financial aid for their college tuition. The costs of education in the United States are constantly on the rise. Many families struggle daily to put their children through college. To ease the financial burden, Downtown NYC Investing offers quarterly $500 scholarships to students who are currently in college or planning to attend college this upcoming semester.

*Essay Question:*
To be considered for the scholarship, students must submit a 1000+ word essay answering the following question:

Many students graduate from high school with little-to-no knowledge about money, banking, and finance. How can young adults take steps toward learning more about finance to increase the quality of their lives?

The deadlines for our quarterly scholarships are the following dates: 3/30, 6/30, 9/30, and 12/30. One week following the deadline, we will announce the winner of the scholarship on our Facebook page and share their essay.

*Application:*
Ask for their full name, email address, phone number, where they are currently enrolled, where they will be attending the following semester, their area of study, and a place to submit their essay.

Pro-Tip: I highly recommend using Gravity Forms to create the application.

If you aren't using Gravity Forms already, you should start now. **It's an extremely powerful tool** that integrates seamlessly with WordPress and allows you to create simple forms for lead captures, job applications, guest blog submissions, or in this case, scholarship applications.

Once you sign up for Gravity Forms you will not know how you ever lived without it, I promise.

**Step 2:** Type the following into Google's search bar: Inurl:. edu "scholarships"

**Step 3:** Click on each search result and find an email address for the scholarship department of that particular college.

**Step 4:** Send a nice, personalized email to the scholarship department telling them about your scholarship offer, why you are doing it (to help kids - not build SEO, of course ;), and include the link to your scholarship page.

**Step 5:** Repeat steps 2 through 4 for all the search results for the first five or so pages of Google. *The more the merrier.* **Every email you send is a potential high-quality .edu backlink to your website.** Spend time on this and it will be well worth the effort.

**Step 6:** Try to keep track of who responds to your emails. Make sure to thank them.  Give anyone who hasn't responded a few weeks to respond, as those departments can get extremely busy during peak enrollment seasons.

If it has been three weeks since you've heard a response

from a particular school, first check their scholarship page to see if they listed you without saying anything. If they have, great, send them a "thank you," email. If they haven't, politely inquire about the status.

**Step 7:** Repeat step 6 until you've got a good 20+ .edu backlinks. As always, the more, the merrier. Remember, in the end it's only potentially a $2000 annual investment (or however much you decide to offer for your annual scholarship.)

Schools across the US can apply to your scholarship, and in the end, every quarter there will only be one winner. **Also making it annual, at the very least, ensures your scholarship offer stays on the .edu pages every year.**

# Infographics

## What are Infographics?

Infographics are visual representations of processes, information, or data depicted in charts, graphs, images, or diagrams.

## Why Use Infographics?

They are an extremely easy and great way to create backlinks to your website. Infographics are liked and shared THREE TIMES more than any other form of content. Since humans are visual creatures, visual representations of abstract data, concepts, and ideas resonate well with us.

**A single, high-quality infographic has the potential to create hundreds of backlinks to your website.**

They are a very unique source of backlinks that *most people don't bother with because they believe it is hard to create infographics.*

## How to Create and Use Infographics:

**Step 1:** Choose one of the articles you created in the Content Strategy section. I recommend starting off with your most-searched long tail keyword to ensure the largest exposure possible.

Let's just say your keyword was "how the banking system creates money."

**Step 2:** If you followed all the steps in the Content Strategy section of this book, you should have created a bullet list or short summary of your article and placed it at the beginning of your article.

If you did, great! Copy this list or summary to use in the next step. If you did not, then create a bullet list of your article. In this case, "how the banking system creates money," you want to use the least amount of words possible.

**Successful infographics have a lot of blank, or white space, and feature comprehensive designs and pictures - not a lot of words.** Once you have a short, bullet list of your article, move on to the next step.

**Step 3:** Post a job listing for "High-Quality Infographic Design" on Upwork. Ask the potential freelancers to attach previous infographics they have created or a link to their infographic portfolio. I recommend offering around $100-$250 for a decent infographic.

Personally, I prefer offering around $250+ for higher-quality ones, but do what your budget will allow.

If you want to try your hand at creating an infographic your-self, I recommend checking out Visme. It's a free visual media creator with infographic templates you can use.

**Step 4:** Choose one of the freelancers who applied for the job by browsing the infographics in their portfolios. The most successful infographics feature more images and visuals.

*They aren't crowded or cramped with information or visuals and typically have ample amounts of white or blank space to balance the design.* Whichever designer you choose, make sure you convey the specs of the design to them.

Do a Google search for "best infographics" and take notice of their commonalities.

**Step 5:** Once you hire the freelancer to design the infographic, provide them with the bullet list you created summarizing your content. They will use this to create the infographic.

If you have an idea or concept of how you want the info-graphic to look, *make sure you tell the freelancer.* If you have no idea what you want it to look like at all, *tell them that too.*

They can usually come up with something decent on their own using a bullet list of the content.

**Step 6:** When the infographic is complete, you need to add embed it onto the corresponding content page on your web-site. The best way to do this to ensure the content is share-able and can easily create backlinks for you is by generating an image embed code.

Here is a link to a free embed code generator: https://www. siegemedia.com/embed-code-generator. Follow the link, choose the "Embed Image" tab, and simply fill in all of the blank fields with the appropriate data.

## Embed Code Generator

Embed Image  Embed Video  FAQ

### Settings

| | | | |
|---|---|---|---|
| Site Name: | YourDomain.com | Embed Box Width: | 540px |
| Post URL: | https://domain.com/post-url/ | Embed Box Height: | 100px |
| Image URL: | https://domain.com/image.jpg | | |
| Image Alt: | Infographic Name | | |
| Width of Image: | 540px | | |
| Height of Image: | Leave empty to keep proportion | | |

**Use This Code**

```
<h3>Share this Image On Your Site</h3><textarea
onclick='this.focus();this.select()'
style='width:540px;height:100px'><p><strong>Please include
attribution to site name goes here Here with this graphic.
</strong><br /><br /><a href=''><img src='' alt='' width='''
border='0'/></a></p></textarea>
```

Once you've generated the embed code, use it to place the video on your web page. This embed code will make it extremely easy for users to share your video and create backlinks to your content.

**Step 7:** Share it on your social media channels.

**Step 8:** Submit your infographic on other infographic sharing sites like Visual.ly, Nerdgraph, DailyInfoGraphic, and AmazingInfoGraphics.

**Step 9:** Email other authoritative blogs in your niche and offer the infographic as a guest post. Include a unique description for their site for when they post the infographic. **Do this for multiple sites. Remember, the more links, the merrier.**

**Step 10:** Repeat steps 1 through 9 for any articles that an infographic could represent in an artful way. Again, *I recommend prioritizing them by the number of searches the particular keyword generates per month.* That way, you get more exposure more quickly.

# Toxic Link Removal

## What is Toxic Link Removal?

Toxic link removal involves reviewing the domains and links pointing to your website, determining which ones are "toxic," and removing (or "disavowing") them.

## Why Toxic Links Need to be Removed:

Toxic links can trigger Google penalties and greatly hinder your SEO efforts. Remember, you only want to associate your website with other good, high-quality websites.

Monitoring backlinks to your website is an important step in the SEO process. Toxic links to your website negatively affect your website's ability to rank highly in Google search results. Google wants to know they can trust your website before sending visitors.

Backlinks from spammy websites are an indication to Google that all may not be well with your website. So your SEO strategy will suffer as a result.

## How to Remove Toxic Links:

**Step 1:** Go to your SEMrush dashboard. In the box that says "Backlink Audit," click on "Set up Backlink audit," and choose your website (or "project" as SEMrush refers to it as.)

**Step 2:** A screen similar to the one below will appear. Make the appropriate domain selection for your website, specify your brand name, and click "Domain Categories."

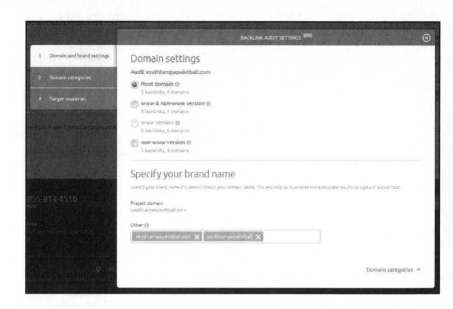

**Step 3:** Select the categories or themes that most closely reflect your website. This will help refine the results and find bad links. Then, click "Target Countries."

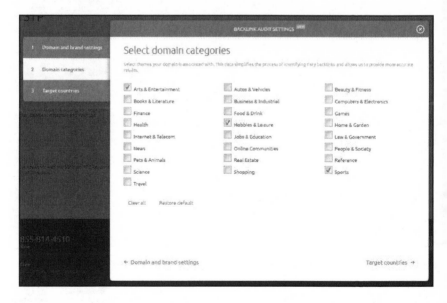

**Step 4:** Type in the countries your website services and click "Start Backlink Audit."

**Step 5:** Connect your Google Search Console property with SEM-rush by clicking on the link provided on the screen that says "1. Go to Google Search Console."

**Step 6:** Click on the property associated with your website. Then click on the cog icon in the top right corner of the screen and choose "Users and Property Owners."

**Step 7:** Click "ADD A NEW USER" under the cog icon.

**Step 8:** Copy and paste the following email address in the "User email" field, with "Full" permission. Click Add and go back to the SEMrush page.

**Step 9:** Click "Check connection and continue." If it worked, great! If not, try again. But it's not necessary to completing the toxic backlink removal. It just takes a few steps out of the process.

## Connect Google Search Console

**How can it help me?**

By integrating your SEMrush account with Google Search Console, you will be able to access extra backlinks for your analysis, get the up-to-date data on disavowed backlinks, and update your Disavow file with just one click.

**Integrate your SEMrush account with Google Search Console**

1. Go to Google Search Console.
2. Share your property with SEMrush email **backlink.audit.pro.13@gmail.com**.
3. Select access type: restricted or full (recommended).
4. Share both http and https versions of your site, if applied.

Important

Google treats www and non-www versions of a website as different sites. If you need to audit each version separately, set up a separate project and a Backlink Audit campaign for each of them.

Show more details ∨

✓ Check connection and continue

**Step 10:** Give it a few minutes or an hour to complete the backlink audit of your website. You will see the following in the top right corner of the Backlink Audit page:

Auditing domain - 63%

**Step 11:** Under the "Audit" tab, click on the "Toxic" tab.

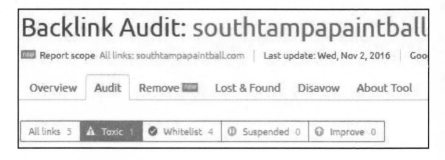

# Backlink Audit: southtampapaintball

🔲 Report scope All links: southtampapaintball.com | Last update: Wed, Nov 2, 2016 | Goo

Overview | Audit | Remove🔲 | Lost & Found | Disavow | About Tool

All links 5 | ⚠ Toxic 1 | ✓ Whitelist 4 | ⓘ Suspended 0 | ⓘ Improve 0

**Step 12:** Check the boxes next to each Toxic link and click "Move to…" and choose "Disavow Domain."

**Step 13:** Click on the "Disavow" tab.

**Step 14:** Click "Export" and save the file somewhere you can easily find it.

**Step 15:** While logged in to your Google Search Console, follow this link: https://www.google.com/webmasters/tools/disavow-links-main

**Step 16:** Choose your website from the list and click "DISAVOW LINKS."

## Disavow links

If you believe your site's ranking is being harmed by low-quality links you do not control, you can ask Google not to take them into account when assessing your site. You should still make every effort to clean up unnatural links pointing to your site. Simply disavowing them isn't enough. More information.

| https://nobsseostrategy.com/ ⬍ | DISAVOW LINKS |
| --- | --- |

**Step 17:** You will see a warning explaining that this feature is advanced and should be used with caution. Disavowing good backlinks could negatively affect your website's performance in Google's search results. Always make sure your disavow list consists of toxic backlinks.

Click "Disavow Links."

**Step 18:** Click "Choose File," and select the disavow file you created from SEMrush in Step 14. Then click "Submit."

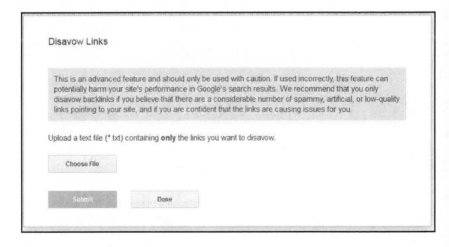

**Step 19:** Check and refresh your Backlink Audit every week or so.

If any new toxic links appear, repeat steps 11 through 18 to update your disavow list.

## Congratulations!

You have completed the backlink strategy for your article. Keep working on expanding your network and sharing your hard work with potential customers on the internet.

# Continued SEO Education
## How to Stay Up to Date on the Ever-Changing SEO Environment

If you have followed the instructions outlined in this book up to this point, you are headed in the right direction. As I've stated multiple times, *keeping the momentum is the most crucial part of the process.*

As 2018 progresses, new information and trends will undoubtedly surface. SEO, like most technology, is on an exponential growth curve, meaning **it's constantly changing and evolving: especially with the implementation of machine learning.**

It's becoming extremely easy to get left in the dust, so one of the most important habits you can develop to maintain momentum is to <u>stay informed with authoritative SEO sources</u>.

I've listed my favorite go-to SEO sources below. I recommend subscribing to their mailings lists and YouTube channels, following them on Facebook, or any other online avenue you consume news and media through.

*Make it a habit to check in weekly or monthly to keep your finger on the SEO pulse. It's the best way to stay ahead and give your content an edge.*

**Follow these sources and check in with them monthly to stay up to date on the latest and greatest SEO developments:**

- <u>Backlinko – backlinko.com</u>
- <u>Moz – moz.com</u>
- <u>Search Engine Land – searchengineland.com</u>
- <u>SERoundtable – seroundtable.com</u>
- <u>Google Search Console – support.google.com/webmasters</u>

# Congratulations!

You have completed the 2018 SEO No-Bullsh*t Strategy! Rinse and repeat for all of your web content and watch your content percolate to the top of Google's search results!

If you would like more assistance with your SEO efforts, feel free to reach out to me at NoBSSEOStrategy.com!

Made in the USA
Lexington, KY
17 August 2019